Hannah's Story

I have set before you life and
death, blessing and cursing;
therefore choose life, that
thou and thy seed may live.

—*Deuteronomy 30:19*

Hannah Kalajian

Foreword by ROBERT MIRAK

Hannah's Story

ESCAPE FROM GENOCIDE IN TURKEY

TO SUCCESS IN AMERICA

BY HANNAH KALAJIAN

As told to Bernadine Sullivan

ARMENIAN HERITAGE PRESS

National Association for Armenian Studies and Research
Belmont, Massachusetts

ARMENIAN HERITAGE PRESS
National Association for Armenian Studies and Research, Inc.
395 Concord Ave., Belmont, Mass. 02178
Printed in the United States of America

Library of Congress Cataloging-in-Publication Data

Kalajian, Hannah, 1910–
  Hannah's story: escape from genocide in Turkey to success in
America / by Hannah Kalajian; as told to Bernadine Sullivan;
foreword by Robert Mirak.
        p.   cm.
  1. Kalajian, Hannah, 1910–   .   2. Armenian Americans —
Biography.
I. Sullivan, Bernadine.   II. National Association for Armenian
Studies and Research (U.S.)   III. Title.
E184.A7K35   1990
973'.049199202 — dc20
[B]   90 – 35104
                                                       CIP

ISBN 0–935411–08–9 (cloth)

*I*n memory of the victims of the
Genocide of the Armenians in Turkey
on this 75th commemorative year
(1915–1990)

and

For my children
Cohar, Jack, Carol, and all their progeny

so that memories will live

Contents

Photographs

Foreword

Hannah Kalajian's stirring and poignant memoir, *Hannah's Story*, is a portrait in microcosm of the Armenian-American experience. Born in Düzce, Turkey, in the latter days of the Ottoman Empire, Hannah saw her happy childhood abruptly shattered by the genocide of the Armenian population carried out by the Turkish government during and immediately following World War I. Uprooted and forced to flee from home, Hannah found her way to an orphanage in Constantinople, then to a refugee settlement in Beirut, and finally, after a lonely sea journey, to the home of an older sister in New York City.

In America Hannah experienced the warmth of her sister's home, the challenges of an urban industrial society, and (at times) the alienation of the immigrant in America and the pressure to assimilate; she changed her name from Heranoush Gartazoghian to Hannah Reader. Then followed marriage within the ethnic group, raising a family, financial struggles, and final successs.

Her story, told here in a straightforward, gripping narrative, was repeated with countless variations by the thousands of others between 1890 and 1924 who formed the first generation of Armenian Americans. The story of these pioneers forms the indispensable background for understanding the present-day Armenian-American community.

Hannah's story has other significance as well. In

Hannah's lifetime, the United States became an economic powerhouse whose achievements astonished the world. And an important role in that development was the contribution of individual entrepreneurs—native-born and immigrant—who used their skills and ingenuity to amass wealth and productivity for themselves and the new economic giant.

What inspired and drove these often unknown and inconspicuous individuals and families to concentrate all their energies, even risking their health and their savings, to achieve success? What chemistry took place between individual aspiration and American opportunity to generate the battalions of new entrepreneurs who turned out the goods and services which became national products? The answers to these questions, which the poorer and less-developed countries of the world now long to know, are revealed in the autobiography of Hannah Kalajian.

Finally, Hannah's story is the chronicle of personal triumph over adversity. Repeatedly, she and her family endure sickness, disappointments, and failures that would daunt most others. And the narrative is replete with her struggles, pain, weariness, exhaustion, and moments of depression. But the will to survive and to overcome adversity dominates; the overwhelming theme is one of optimism and strength.

Hannah Kalajian's life story is an inspiring example of one person's indomitable persistence and fortitude. Armenians and non-Armenians alike will find it a powerful and engrossing account.

ROBERT MIRAK*

*Author of *Torn Between Two Lands: Armenians in America, 1890 to World War I* (Cambridge, Mass.: Harvard University Press, 1983).

Acknowledgments

I have been blessed with family and friends who have freely and generously given me help and encouragement when I needed it most, not only to achieve personal success but to satisfy my compelling desire to tell my story. Without them this book would not have been written. I am grateful to them all, but especially to the following:

My dear children, Cohar, Jack, and Carol, and my nephew Marcel;

My collaborator, Bernadine Sullivan, who took the raw facts of my life and breathed dramatic life into them;

My editor, Barbara J. Merguerian, whose patience and enthusiasm made everything easier, and the National Association for Armenian Studies and Research, for making arrangements for the publication of this book.

HANNAH KALAJIAN

I also feel indebted to many people, especially to my good friend Hannah Kalajian, for her patience in searching and re-searching her memory for the facts of her remarkable life; to my husband Paul, for being "first reader" and best critic; to my typist Joan Graham, who thinks as well as she types; and to Cohar Bartlett, for being a great facilitator.

BERNADINE SULLIVAN

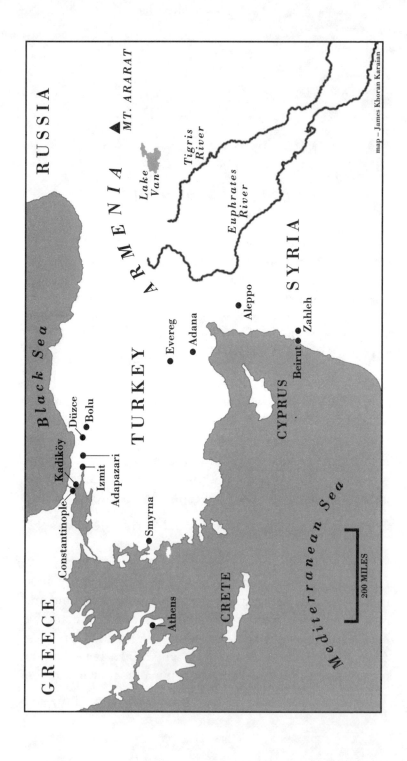

map – James Khoran Karaian

Prologue

THE autumn leaves dance like whirling dervishes outside my living-room windows. The morning sun reaches in to warm my body. Later today I'll put on a woolen coat and hat and take a walk. Autumn dies all too soon in this New England town.

I pace, I can't sit still. I am restless, anxious, even a little tired already. When will she arrive, the interviewer, I wonder? She should be here soon, and I will begin to tell her the story of my life . . . a long journey of the mind, each year a bead to be held and rolled in the fingers, then released.

I do want this story told, but it will be very hard for me. What is it, an old woman's conceit? A wish to live forever? I don't think so. I want my children, and their children, to know the path I traveled, although there is no way to tell it all, to relive it for someone else. How do you explain that dreams can rise out of squalor and death? How is courage born of bitterness?

The doorbell shrills into my reverie.

"Your home, how lovely it is! And you—you look so well, Hannah," murmurs the interviewer.

"Yes, I'm fine. You'll have coffee? Shall we sit in here?"

It's true, the house is lovely, as my guest says. It's strange to think that now I can have any luxury I want. I can feed my body the finest, the freshest, the best. But it means little. There is nothing I want except this: to bear witness to my own life, to be a part of the story of my people.

1
Düzce

THE ancient village of Düzce, about a hundred miles east of Istanbul, still appears on this modern map of Turkey. You see, there, close to the Black Sea? A large river feeds the fertile plain that borders the town, and in the distance southward the purple mountains rise.

Near the close of the nineteenth century, my parents chose Düzce as a good place to settle down and raise a family. They would be reasonably safe here from the wrath of the Turkish government. My father had worked in Constantinople, as Istanbul was called then, where the eyes of foreign governments watched the relationships between the Turks and their ethnic subjects. Düzce, while close enough for protection, was more peaceful than the raucous metropolis; yet here, too, the wealthy Turks would eagerly patronize the Armenian tradesmen.

My parents had wandered far from their birthplace, in Evereg, in central Turkey. Evereg lies near the heart of old Armenia, where the Tigris and Euphrates flow, the land of Mt. Ararat, and the fabled site of the Garden of Eden.

My mother's father was an honored priest of Evereg. When he gave his daughter Cohar to young Mateos Gartazoghian in marriage, he didn't know that he would soon embrace her in farewell. Like so many other merchants and tradesmen, Mateos had to look beyond Evereg for work. The venerable priest comforted himself with the thought that his daughter might be safer far away from the area of Evereg, where so many pogroms against the Armenians had struck in the past.

So Mateos and Cohar chose Düzce, and at first fortune was kind. Mateos became a prosperous meat merchant. In 1910 he welcomed into the world his fourth daughter. I was that child. They called me Heranoush, "sweet-fire" in Armenian.

I search my memory, back, back over more than seven decades, to capture the first fuzzy image of those childhood years. The image sharpens.

"Heranoush! Heranoush!"

My mother bends over me. I crawl slowly out of my warm quilt. She slides my best dress — whoosh — over my head. It smells clean. She ties a red sash around my waist.

"Today," she says, "you will have your picture taken!"

Picture? What is a "picture," I wonder.

"And you will see a wedding!"

She does not explain further, but she is smiling. She doesn't smile often, so I hug her, and run off to play, carefully, because I know I must stay clean today and because I am wearing my soft leather "Sunday" shoes.

All day people arrive, in fancy clothes.

"Say hello to your cousin, Heranoush!"

"This is your aunt, and here is your cousin Sarkis . . ."

An old woman sits me down, and before I know what is happening, she cuts my blond hair so short that my curls bounce up and down.

"Ooh!" I laugh, shaking my head.

"Better for the picture . . . ," she clucks.

Soon a tall man with a big black box tells me to stand

still and smile. Click!

"Now one with your daddy and mama!" Click! Click!

I can't remember ever seeing the pictures. But the memory of that day, the laughter, the mysterious ceremony, my mother's face, my soft leather moccasins— it is a good memory.

*

*   *

I am five years old the day my father brings the camel and gives me a ride. By this time I know many things about our family and about Düzce.

I know that I have a big sister, Dikranouhi, and an even older sister called Nazeli, who has a husband already and two babies. Nazeli and her family are rich, my mother says. "Rich" I don't understand, but I have seen the shop they own, in the long street of shops, where golden necklaces sway and diamond rings sparkle brighter than the sun itself. I also have another sister not too much bigger than I am, although she tells me she is eleven. Her name is Haigouhi. She is beautiful and kind. She talks to me when no one else will. Haigouhi tells me that our baby brother Norayr is a very special person because he is a boy. Our mother and father wept with joy when Norayr was born, especially because a long time ago when God sent the first baby to our mother and father, that one was a boy, too, but he died when he was still an infant. I don't ask Haigouhi what "died" means because she looks very sad when she tells me this story.

I know other things, too. I know we are not Turks, because they live on the other side of the town. The Turks are fierce. They call us *giavors*, which means "heathens," but mama says we are Christians. I am afraid of the Turks. Haigouhi says we are Armenians, and the Turks hate us because we are not Moslems like they are.

But I was going to tell you about my father and the camel. My father is a butcher. Everyone in Düzce buys meat from him. Even the Turks work for him.

His shop is in the big marketplace. It is a wonderland for Haigouhi and me. All across the front hang huge chunks of camel meat drying in the sun. Inside, the odor of spices tickles your nose. The workers will add these delicious spices when they dry the meat to make *soujoukh* and *basterma*. The whole shop smells heavenly.

I wake up warm and drowsy on this summer day. Where is everyone? I have slept like a lazy bug because it is so hot, I guess. Mama has told me about the houses in Evereg, where she grew up. Their roofs were flat and covered with a thick layer of smooth dried mud, and on hot summer nights the whole family would sleep up on the roof. What fun that would be!

"Come, Heranoush, quickly!" Haigouhi sounds excited, a happy kind of excited.

I scramble out of bed. There, coming up the street from the marketplace, is my father, pulling a dusty camel by a long rope. The poor creature has clumps of ragged hair, his humps quiver and sway, and his eyes roll wildly. Someone has slung a bright red rug over his back.

"Your turn, Heranoush!" shouts my father. He taps the camel's leg, and when the animal sinks to his knees my father tosses me like a feather in his strong arms, up, up onto that red carpet, and away we go, parading down the street, all the way to the river bridge and back again. I can touch the branches of the trees from my high seat! I'm not afraid, because my father is leading the camel. I am a little shy, with the older children all staring up at me, and maybe a little sad, too, because I know this camel is going to become delicious spicy meat in the shop very soon, but mostly I feel happy and important.

Hannah's father, Mateos
Gartazoghian, in Evereg,
early 1900s.

Mateos Gartazoghian's
brother and family about
1912, in a small village near
Düzce.

Hannah's grandfather, the priest Yeghishe Der
Yeghishian (seated, center), with some members of his
family, in Evereg, 1911. Seated, his daughter Dirouhi
Batzanian (left) and his wife, holding grandson Yervant
(right). Standing, left to right, Dirouhi's son John
Batzanian, her daughter-in-law Zarouhi, and son Levon
Batzanian (Zarouhi's husband).

I have been telling you this because the good memories were gone so quickly and our lives were so soon to become shadowed and desperate. Later, after our flight from Düzce, I would dream of the good smells of home, the *bulghur* (cracked wheat kernels) cooking, the big iron pans of *parag hats* (Armenian cracker bread) baking over the open fire, the apricots and raisins spread out to dry. I would remember the green park across from the circle of Armenian houses, where we would run and play our singing games under the fragrant mulberry trees and the walnut trees. Each family had marked out a section of the park by hanging a children's swing from a favorite tree, and we would all race to claim "our own" swings.

And I would think about our Armenian church, its deep-shaded stone arches, the cool silence inside, the mysterious paintings covering the walls; I remember that my mother and I would carry our cushions in, kneel silently, and then my mother would whisper to me proudly that my grandfather was a much-honored priest in the city of Evereg.

*

* *

It is 1915. I am not yet six years old when my world suddenly darkens. The Turkish soldiers have come and snatched my father, and many other young Armenian men, to "serve" in the army.

"To work like a slave for them, not to be a soldier!" screams my mother, crying and tearing at her hair. "They don't take the ones who can bribe the officers! The ones they need for themselves, like the doctors, they don't take!"

People mutter to each other about "the European war," "the Germans," and "the Allies." The Turks turn fierce eyes on us.

My father's shop is closed, and all the meat disappears with the soldiers as they sweep on to another town.

My mother is very sad. Once she loved to sing, mostly the hymns from the church mass; she knew them all from beginning to end. But the songs have gone. To keep our family together she works in the tobacco fields now, with the other women and the older children. They trudge home at sunset with their hands stained black with tar from the tobacco plants. Nothing will remove the stains. Sunburned faces, blackened hands, and work, work, but never enough money to keep stomachs filled, the house warm in winter, the clothing decent.

I see mama early in the morning bending over a huge pot of boiling water, washing clothes to earn a few extra *ghurush* (pennies) before she goes to the fields. And I sense that she is giving up hope for my father to return. I listen to the village women muttering that "the army starves them," "our men are not allowed to fight like soldiers," ". . . they are worked to death like beasts!"

Other rumors buzz around us like angry bees.

"The Turks are killing our people again . . ."

". . . Armenian villages, even cities, where everyone is driven out . . ."

"The women violated, and babies dying at the breasts of dead mothers . . ."

"The houses burned . . ."

". . . a death march to the desert . . ."

Terrible rumors, but the truth is much worse. In a way it is a blessing that the whole truth filters in slowly. How would we have had the will to resist, the temerity to hope, if we had known that the Turkish Minister of War Enver Pasha had decreed that *all* the Armenians in Turkey must be exterminated? That the government had ordered the genocide of the Armenians by means of deportation, forced marches, starvation, or slaughter? Thank God we don't know until later that our people who live to the east, including the Evereg region where my father and mother were married and where all our relatives lived, have been driven by the whips of the gendarmes along a hellish road, all the way to the Syrian desert, where the pitiful few who survived were now perishing daily. Armenia, the first country in history to declare itself a Christian nation, was facing extinction, while World War I claimed the spotlight of the news. Slaughter, slavery, the capture of our females for Turkish harems, all this we had suffered many times over. What we didn't comprehend at first was the magnitude of this effort or the crazed abandon of the uncontrollable hordes who carried out Enver Pasha's edict.

If you are a child, like me, however, you push away the rumors. Maybe they will go away, like the morning mist lifting from our valley. Meanwhile, life surges within me. I'm old enough for school, where each day brings magical new skills. One reality threatens the magic. I have a mysterious ailment which pounces on me without warning. I begin to shake with fever; my body collapses like a rag doll. So many times I must stay home from school. What is wrong with me? My illness, which pursues me all my life, probably arises from the open cesspools and cisterns which sit in our yards. Could the malnutrition from which most of us suffer make our bodies easy targets for germs? Who knows? The word "malaria" is not in our vocabularies.

Fortunately I am a determined child, endlessly curious, driven to find solutions, not dead-ends. So I follow my mother and sisters like a pet lamb, imitating their skills and getting my small fingers into cooking pots and sewing baskets. Then two events happen which make me glad I am old enough to help.

First, my sister Dikranouhi has been taken into the home of one of the few wealthy families left in Düzce, to help with the children. I miss her so much—she is a second mother to me. But her going becomes a blessing. Every few days she appears on our doorstep; always she brings us food, and sometimes money. My dear sister, you are keeping us alive.

Secondly, an Armenian man has set his eyes on my beautiful sister Haigouhi. She is now perhaps fourteen. I am about eight. It does no good to argue against the engagement. He is one of the wild ones, like the Turkish men, who will carry her off by force if she resists. This is well known. It has happened before. So it is agreed.

He brings her gifts. Strange presents, like the exotic salted fish which rests in her drawer where I can see and smell its intriguing odor but I must not touch it. Much too soon Haigouhi leaves our home to marry this man, and to have a son by him. A son should make any mother proud, but Haigouhi's lovely eyes have a sadness which never leaves. I will tell you more of her story later.

There are only three of us left in our house now—my mother, Norayr, and I. Word reaches us that our father is dead. Beaten and driven, he starved to death in an army labor camp. The news stabs at my heart, but I feel no pain. Nor do I see my mother cry. In a village where so many men have gone, the women pass each other with a shrug of the shoulders; their eyes exchange dark, familiar sorrows. They hold themselves tight and rock in the silent nights. But tears are useless.

Our older sister Nazeli has moved to Constantinople, where she and her husband own a profitable jewelry shop in the huge Covered Bazaar.

"Mother," I ask more than once, "why are we so poor when Nazeli is rich? Why does she not help us?"

"Sh-h, little one," she frowns.

But one day she squats beside me on the dry ground. "I will tell you something, Heranoush," she says, beginning to trace a picture in the dirt with a small stick. "See these steps I am drawing? Now on the bottom step there is Nazeli, you see? On the next step is her husband; on the next her sister-in-law. On the next is the sister-in-law's husband. On the top step is Nazeli's mother-in-law. The mother-in-law rules the household, and your sister is at the bottom. She does not command; she exists to obey. Do you understand?"

Well, I understand enough so that I ask no more questions. I put Nazeli out of my mind.

Besides, my duties are many these days. I clean and sew, and I cook the pilaf, which we make mostly from the wheat we are allowed to scoop up from the fields after the harvest. During the summer months I carry pilaf out to my mother where she toils in the tobacco fields. Sometimes, when I see how tired she is, I snatch the hoe from her hands and hack fiercely at the earth.

Everywhere I go I must also watch over Norayr. I love him, even though my eight-year-old mind realizes that he is more precious to my mother than I am, since he is a boy and must be fostered at all costs. Children accept these things, and I am a very practical child.

When the tobacco harvest is in, I help the women pile it into the huge drying shed. For days we string the leaves on endless long lines. I love to watch the way the sun turns the leaves to amber gold.

It was just such a late summer day, with the shed full of radiant color, when the skies fell in on us.

2

Flight

THE year is 1920. I am ten years old. Our village is peacefully off guard. The terrible pogroms of 1915–1916 have relaxed. A few of our men have straggled back from the war. We in Düzce count it a blessing that we lived close enough to Constantinople to have escaped the horror and death that the Armenians suffered in central and eastern Turkey. Just as my father had reasoned, American and European eyes and ears had monitored the Turkish madness from the safety of Constantinople. We had lived under their protective wingspread, or so we imagined, until today.

Early this morning a man slipped secretly into our village with an ominous message. The man is exhausted and filthy. He has run to us from Bolu, a town a dozen kilometers to the east.

"The Turks!" he gasps. "The Turkish gendarmes . . . !"

They came from nowhere, he says. They have pillaged his town, slashing, raping, robbing, and killing. Worst of all, he sobs, they forced all the Armenians they could find into the church and then burned it down.

Now there is nothing left but corpses, and the smell of burning flesh and the moans of the dying. All day and night this man survived by hiding in a cesspool. Today he has risked his life to warn us that we are to be next. Our own village of Düzce will have blood running in the streets; our only hope is to leave immediately.

Panic! No time for preparations. Run! Run! But where? How? My mother drops the stick with which she has been stirring the clothes in a huge pot. Where is Norayr? Where is my brother? My mother and I stagger through the streets and shops, calling his name. Thank God, here he is down by the bridge with another family. No time now for packing food, clothing, or blankets. Hurry! We race to join the sad procession leaving the town, searching for our relatives as we go. Finally we are a frightened group together: my mother, Norayr, and I; and ah, thank God again, there are Haigouhi and her baby, John.

I should tell you at this point that Haigouhi's husband has left her months before "to find work in Constantinople," perhaps to send for her later—who knows? For now, it is enough that she is with us. Are you wondering what has happened to Dikranouhi? She is lucky, I think. Last year she went to Constantinople to work for a family there.

Where will we go? An entire village on the run? To Constantinople? But how will we find the way? How will we escape the angry swords of the Turkish gendarmes? The sun sets and despair hovers over our heads like an impatient vulture.

One small miracle has happened, however, and the news filters back to us as we shiver under the cold sky. A Cherkess man has volunteered to show us the way to Constantinople, through the mountains. The Cherkess are a Moslem people who are fiercely independent. This noble man will prove to be true to his word. Later we will learn of the lavish honors he will receive from our patriarch and others for saving our villagers and also the hordes who joined us along the way on that desperate one-hundred-mile flight to Constantinople.

We stumble along without food and without clothing except what we are wearing. Avoiding cities and towns, we hide often by day high up among rocks and bushes on the mountainsides.

Terrible rumors snap at our heels.

"The Turks are paying a bounty for every Armenian head!"

"They do such things to our women . . .! One woman, a young virgin who tried to resist—they cut off her breasts . . ."

". . . and babies, it is said they toss the infants back and forth on the ends of their scimitars, for sport!"

My mother turns our heads from such talk.

"Say your prayers and trust in God," she says.

For my part, I try to help God out by scrounging a bit of bread here, or a handful of raisins there, from some more fortunate family group. Meanwhile my sister Haigouhi puts one foot in front of the other, like a sleepwalker, and when baby John whimpers she seems not to notice.

Our mother, who never complains, makes an attempt to cheer us, at sundown. First she sets an imaginary pot over an imaginary fire. Then she stirs and stirs as if there is something cooking.

"Now the pilaf is cooking," she croons. "It will be ready soon! How good it will taste! Can you smell it?"

We sit on the cold ground, hugging our knees, hypnotized. I am sure I can smell the hot pilaf and see the glow of the flames. Somehow it is easier to go to sleep with the taste of home in our heads.

Is it the third night, or the fourth, when we hear the

gunfire? Are the shots above us? From the valley? How close? No one knows. But everyone scatters blindly. The last sunset light fades and darkness drops on us. Is this the end? Where is my family? Can we not at least die together?

What's that ahead of me? Shadows bunch up. And a new sound. The ripple of water over rocks. Now I can make out mama, and Norayr. Good. Can we get across the stream? Maybe we'll be safe on the other side.

"The Cherkess man says we must cross. Come ..." Mama pulls at me and Norayr.

"Come on, Haigouhi! Hurry!" I can barely see my sister, holding baby John and staring at the dark river.

Good, she's starting across. But suddenly, like a crazy woman, Haigouhi thrusts the baby from her chest and hurls him into the swift, gray water. His little body rolls and bobs between the rocks, disappears, and comes up again.

Quickly my mother, with a wild cry, lunges for the baby, slips, recovers, reaches out again, grabs his curly hair, then an arm, and—finally—she has him! Many hands wrap around them to hold them up. Together we slide and stagger our way to the opposite shore. Someone closes a shawl around the dripping child.

All at once we realize that Haigouhi still stands midstream. She is screaming over and over, until her voice dies to a rasping whisper, "The Turks will get him! They'll kill him! Better to let him die now! Better for him to be dead!"

My mother reaches her arms out to Haigouhi: "Come, little one, it's all right. He's safe. Come on now, that's right."

Her voice is low and comforting. Haigouhi inches across the stream, bent like an old woman.

I look at my sister. I have never before wept so much in my heart for anyone. But even in that moment something in me clamors, no, no! Life is better than death! Never give up!

Now a pelting rain digs at our shadows, and the night turns so black I can't see anyone. Finally, wet to the skin, I sink down behind a bush. Hours, or so it seems, crawl by. Insects feed greedily on my flesh. I am alone, too terrified to pray, hardly breathing. Suddenly something moves close to my hiding place. Shadows. They whisper hoarsely to one another. My heart dies in my throat. Someone clutches me by the shoulders. A-a-ach! But they are only villagers whom I know! From Düzce! Thank you, God. Thank you, St. Gregory.

"Your mother is frantic, Heranoush! Come follow us," they say.

"But the Turks—?"

"A false alarm, we think. At any rate, too far away now for us to worry about any more. And look! The dawn is coming up. See?"

And so family groups form again, embrace, and go on. It is good just to be alive.

Day by day we creep through the mountains. We have passed Adapazari, Izmit, and other smaller villages. We are joined by additional refugees along the way. Some have food, and a blanket or two. Some have gold pieces sewn into their clothes. Once in a while Armenians from the villages below smuggle bread to us. When we can go far enough down into the valleys, we find fruit trees. When we can't find herbs, we eat grass.

Our senses are dulled by our woes: the old and sick who must be carried on the backs of relatives, the lack of privacy for even the most private of bodily functions, the families that refuse to share, the merciless attacks of insects, the nightmare fears that turn young faces old.

But finally we pass the town of Kadiköy, and on the twentieth day our ragged multitude straggles into the bedlam and the magnificence of Constantinople.

Forgetting the journey, enraptured by the pointed spires, the minarets, the great Hagia Sophia, and the Bosporus bridge in the morning sun, I dart here and there like a wild rabbit. My mother, however, knows that the struggle is far from over.

3

Constantinople

W E mill about the city, confused and tired, for many hours. Then a message races up and down our ranks. "The church! The church will give us shelter!" Someone up front guides us toward a large stone church. The familiar lettering in front of the building tells us it is an Armenian church.

We crowd into every corner of the cool, vaulted interior. It is beautiful. I stare at the gilded painted walls and decide that the figures there welcome us in spite of our dirt and misery. The church will be our home for several days. Miraculously we are fed by various relief agencies. Remembering this now, I am glad that I had no idea then of the two years of hardship and loneliness that lay ahead for me.

My mother has gone to the Covered Bazaar to find Nazeli and her husband in their jewelry shop. The Bazaar in Constantinople—who has not heard of it? The first of its kind in the world, it is said, a building huge beyond belief, where you can find anything, or anyone, you want, from spies to spices to diplomats. I must stay behind with my brother. Some day, I vow, I will see this Bazaar.

Bad news. Nazeli can do nothing for us. But it is no

more than we expected. Mother is resourceful. She will work at something. So we join the hillside chaos of refugees; we scrounge for a bit of wood, a space of our own.

Then my mother tells me what is going to happen to me, her youngest daughter. I will go to an orphanage; I will be "safe" there and not a burden. Norayr will stay with my mother. Well, what did I think her choice would be? A male child over a daughter, of course.

The orphanage hides behind ten-foot walls. Inside, the bare ground surrounds a multi-level building that holds hundreds of Armenian girls, of all ages. Except for a long porch on one side, the structure is grim and functional. My mother cries with me as she tries to say good-bye.

"Look, Heranoush, my sweet daughter, I have a present for you—here, take it." She stretches out her hand to me. Lying on her palm, a dark, sculptured French chocolate sits in its brown plaited wrapper. I hide it carefully in the pocket of my slip. The intoxicating fragrance stays on my fingertips. Mother tucks my bundle of ragged clothes under my arm. Then she is gone.

The crowded orphanage is a strange place, full of rules; yet we have hours of idleness, to do nothing, to be nothing. On the first day an older girl, maybe fourteen, becomes my assigned guardian. Her behavior is erratic, sometimes moody and critical, sometimes far away. Does she live in a nightmare of remembered horror? What has she suffered? Little conversation passes between us. But she follows me like a shadow.

The big girl pulls me toward the dining room. "Quick! Get in line—take a plate!"

Onto each dish plops a mound of macaroni, followed by a drizzle of evil-smelling rancid oil. I gag on the first spoonful.

"Swallow it!" hisses my shadow. "It's all you'll ever get—!"

Mercifully, I don't believe her. But I will find out that on every day of the two years I spend in this place the macaroni and rancid oil will appear on my plate as surely as the rising of the sun. Eat or starve. You must learn quickly, Heranoush, I caution myself, or you will sink and drown here.

After "dinner" I find my cot in the big open dormitory. I stow my possessions under the mattress and lie wide awake, battered by the sounds, the cries, the struggles, and the knocking about of more seasoned, tougher inmates. Finally, in the darkness, I inch my hand down into the pocket of my slip, where my treasure lies. I have the candy in my hand. How velvety it is, how softly moist! I want to pop it into my mouth immediately. But instead I slide it back into its hiding place.

Days later I decide the time has come. I bite into the rich chocolate. I savor it, roll it to and fro behind my closed lips, in the silent dark of the dormitory. I let the sweet juices caress my throat. When the last bit is gone, I hold the little paper cup to my nose. The fragrance is still there. I fold the wrapper and tuck it into my pocket. Thereafter, on every lonely night, I hold that paper cup to my nose and whisper my mother's name.

Once in a while my mother trudges the miles and hills to visit me. One time she brings a pretty box, "to keep your own things in . . . ," she smiles. I have observed that most girls have found hiding places for their precious belongings. I scoot about, searching. Aha, the perfect spot: down in the basement of the building, a niche in the corner where two walls come together. No one will discover my box! A few days later it disappears. Was it my shadow, the big girl? I don't know. How will I survive in this prison where the older girls prey on the younger? Yet there are many here who are smaller and more vulnerable than I am. I finger the chocolate wrapper in my pocket, and lift up my head.

Life settles into a pattern. On Sundays we march across the street, rows upon rows of us, to the Armenian church. We sing hymns, and some comfort filters into my soul.

One Sunday, as we sing in the great open space before the altar, I recognize one of the priests.

"You are from Düzce, from my own village!" My brain shouts it at him. "Don't you know me? I'm Heranoush Gartazoghian, the butcher's daughter!"

I concentrate on his face. But when he looks straight into my eyes, his face is blank. No recognition.

"If you knew that my grandfather was a priest in Evereg, a higher priest than you, then you might smile at me!"

But my grandfather is dead, and we orphans cannot speak or break ranks. Yet I enjoy thinking about the priest, because he is a link to the home we will never see again.

In our free hours we sit in the yard of the orphanage. What does the yard offer? Only the ground we sit on. But something magical springs from the dirt. The older girls are building miniature houses: a bit of moisture, a pile of dirt, and voilà! A tiny dream village takes shape. The builders guard their projects fiercely. We others watch entranced. And so the flat bare earth becomes an endlessly fascinating plaything.

At some time we find out that the older girls know how to make delicate Armenian lace. I think that the lace brings money to the orphanage, maybe even to the artisans themselves. We younger ones hover and strain to see the finger motions. Then we scramble about every day picking up any discarded pieces of thread. Soon we have accumulated enough to practice our own lace-making. We are becoming skillful. A small satisfaction.

I have said that every day is the same here, but this is not quite the truth. One day, one unforgettable day, is different! I can still feel the joy, the freedom of that day. It comes without warning. The orphanage bell wakes us early. We dress, then obey instructions to line up in the yard. We hold out our hands and—wonder of wonders—each hand receives a cluster of romaine lettuce leaves. Armed with this special "lunch," a donation from "outside," we march out the gate and down the street, away from the grim high walls. We are on our way for a day in the park!

The air is clear, the sun shines. We sing our hearts out through the hilly streets, munching our lettuce as we go. No matter that we are thin and ragged; for these precious hours we are free—free to greet the park, to run among the walnut trees, to splash in the fountains, to sit on soft grass and dream. How is it possible to suddenly find such happiness? This is the only day it happens in my two long years in the orphanage, but the joy of it still sings in my soul.

One other routine interrupts the slow procession of days at the orphanage. About once a month we go to the public baths. Does this sound exciting, even sensual? It isn't. It is rather an endurance contest. The baths are cold and dismal. We sit on clammy stones and pour pots of water over each other; then we march back shivering in our thin clothing.

After one such ordeal, a few of us contract a communicable disease, never given a name. Fever weakens us; then miserable sores blossom and itch all over our bodies. Quick action follows. A corner of the porch becomes a curtained-off bedroom for the sick group. One bed for six children. At night we shake with the cold. By day we long for escape from our isolation. Our misery terminates in a trip to the basement area of the building. There a grueling treatment awaits us. Our caretakers pour buckets of hot water over us. Then they mercilessly scrub off all our scabs with bristle brushes, until our skin screams with raw wounds. The evil germs, however, have at last departed.

But the baths do provide me, finally, with an upside-down favor. On a particularly chilly afternoon I feel weak and feverish after our trudge back from the baths. By morning my chest hurts. It is hard to breathe. I have been sick many times before. I will get over this. But in a few more days my lungs fill with fluid and my breath fights its way in frantic gasps from my chest. Pneumonia.

"You must take her out of here," they say firmly to my mother. "We have no facilities to care for a child as sick as yours."

So my mother takes me to the hovel she shares with my brother. I exist in a dream world, hardly conscious, certainly not able to rejoice at my deliverance from the institution that has "nurtured" me for two years.

"What shall we do with her?"

"We have no money for doctors . . ."

My mother and a kind neighbor resolutely lift my body, balance it on their crossed arms, and set off for the Red Cross clinic. Somehow they drag themselves and their burden over the miles of steep streets to the clinic.

"You should give her aspirin," says the Red Cross doctor. That's all? After the long miles, the waiting in line? A child near death and aspirin is all they can offer?

Miraculously, however, patience and love and our own brand of Armenian stubbornness pull me through.

"You get better, my darling," croons my mother, "and I will take you to the Bazaar. There I will fill your pockets with *chamich lablaboo*!"

She and I finally did get to the Bazaar one day. A wonderland beyond all my dreams! I stare upward until I am dizzy at the graceful Gothic arches echoing each other far down the main corridor. I dance from shop to shop. Ah, the shimmering jewels, the silken shawls, the bright carpets, the sweet shops, the baskets of figs and almonds! And oh, the smells . . . the shish kebab, dripping and sizzling over glowing coals! How could one ever forget such a smell? I am so excited and happy that I have no idea whether or not the raisins and roasted chick peas—the promised chamich lablaboo—ever fill my pockets. No matter. I sometimes wonder if this day marks the birth of the entrepreneur within me? I want to own every shop I see. I hate to leave the excitement, the bartering, the jingle of coins, the cries of the vendors.

Reality intrudes a few days later. My mother is cleaning a house, something like a boardinghouse. Several Armenians occupy small rooms there.

One of the Armenians clucks her tongue and says to my mother, "Too bad your Heranoush didn't die . . . there's no food, only suffering. Better for you if she had died!"

Listening in the next room, I feel as if a Turkish dagger has sliced into my heart. If my mother answers, the pain blocks my ears, for I hear nothing. A child carries such wounds forever.

After my recovery, no more orphanage. Thank you, God, for giving me pneumonia! But fate waits just around the corner, ready to strike us with the next crisis.

First let me explain that, during the time when I lived at the orphanage, my dear sister Dikranouhi, the one who worked as a governess, had left Constantinople and had gone to America to marry an Armenian man there. An arranged marriage, to be sure, but to live in the United

Hannah's family in Constantinople, 1922. Seated, center, Hannah's mother, Cohar Gartazoghian. Standing, left to right, brother Norayr, sister Nazeli, sister Haigouhi, and Nazeli's son Hrant. Seated, left to right, Hannah, Haigouhi's son John, and Nazeli's daughter Harantouhi.

Portrait of Hannah's mother, Cohar Gartazoghian, about
1935. Oil painting by Hannah's brother Norayr.

States! How glamorous that must be! We have received a letter from her, all the way from New York City. It contains one hundred and fifty dollars, a fortune surely!

"My dearest family," she writes, "how I miss you! Perhaps it is good that I am so busy with the two babies.

"Are you wondering what the money is for? It is to buy passage for Heranoush to come over to America as soon as she is old enough to travel alone. I miss her so much, and I do need her, mother. I am suffering from a terrible rash on my hands, from the soap or the water, I don't know which. It is hard to take care of babies without putting your hands in water . . ."

Very soon after the first letter comes a second, this one with another fortune—a hundred dollars—inside. Dikranouhi's husband requests that we buy some gold jewelry for her. This is an easy task, and soon a few glittering pieces lie in a velvet cloth, to be admired and then sent to New York City.

But before either I, or the jewelry, start any journey, the unpredictable Turks change the course of our lives again.

"The Turks—the Turks! They have sacked the city of Smyrna!"

"—and the churches, the beautiful churches, burned to the ground!"

Smyrna is a large coastal city to the south.

"If Smyrna is vulnerable, what will be next?"

"Even Constantinople?"

The terrible rumors, the whisperings in the dark, flow through the tenements of the poor and run onward, like a poisoned river, into the gardens of the wealthy. And soon, as on a receding tide, the refugees spew out from the hills, from the ghettos, and from behind garden walls, scrambling to the sea, the jumping off place to yet another harbor of desperate hope.

"If Constantinople, on the very edge of the western world, is not safe, where can we go?"

"Perhaps Europe will see, and help?" But we no longer believe this. How many treaties and agreements to solve the Armenian question have been ignored already, forgotten in favor of more selfish national concerns?

Everyone fears that the tragedy at Smyrna marks the beginning of another holocaust like the terrible years of 1915 and 1916.

The elders speak with sad eyes: "How many of us are there left to kill?"

Old routines of flight return, achingly familiar. Families shrink together in tight circles. Women tie up hasty bundles of dried fruits, bulghur, and tins of foodstuffs. Needles dart back and forth, sewing gold pieces into garment hems and jacket linings. Small boxes hold special treasures. Choices must be made, because boats travel almost anywhere from Constantinople. Some Armenians head for Greece, some for France.

Our own family negotiates passage on the open deck of a working merchant ship bound for Beirut, Lebanon. Even such primitive accommodations will cost us all the money Dikranouhi has sent for my fare to the United States. A pity, but what can we do?

This time we are eight: my mother, Norayr, and I, my sister Nazeli and her husband, their two children, and Nazeli's mother-in-law. Questions spin in my mind, and in the midst of the frenzy of preparations, I capture my mother's attention.

"Why doesn't Nazeli's family give us money for their passage? They are rich, are they not?"

My mother's eyes betray bitterness, but she shrugs and folds her arms around my shoulders, like wings. Her voice is quiet.

"Ah, hush, little one. Nazeli is a woman, and even a rich woman is still a woman who must tread softly in her own home."

Her answer does not satisfy me, but I know better than to argue with my mother. Besides, I have another question to ask.

"We are taking Haigouhi and little John, are we not, Mother?"

Can you see someone grow old before your eyes? I think I see this happen to my mother when I ask about my sister Haigouhi. A grayness, a settling of the features.

"No. She is too poor. And she must await word from her husband. She will not be with us."

We pack and sew in silence. I kept remembering the last time we visited Haigouhi in her tiny house. Her restless husband had by now gone on to Greece to find work. She welcomed us, but when we sat down to share supper with her, she blushed, and desperation showed in her eyes.

"I can only give you these last vegetables from my miserable garden," she stammered. She set down a plate with one sliced onion and a small tomato.

Where would her next food come from? We didn't know. Good-bye, my beautiful sister Haigouhi. May God be merciful.

At the busy harbor we finally locate our boat. We are not the first to arrive. The decks swarm with crying, shouting, shoving bodies. How are we supposed to find room on the deck of this ship? One can hardly move, even to search. The September sun dies across the Bosporus. A cold drizzle starts to fall. I am little, so I wriggle and squirm my way across the slippery deck, straining my eyes in the fading light. Aha! Perfect! I shrill a signal to my mother and soon we are all crowded, like sardines, baggage and all, into a small roofed-over area. A wet, sickish smell rises from a round covered hole in our hideaway. Lift the cover and the green ocean foams beneath. Apparently the ship's garbage leaves the boat daily through this hole. But we are dry. Reason enough to be happy, I think, as sleep weighs upon my eyelids.

Am I only twelve, going on thirteen? Sometimes I feel too old even for laughter; at other times I yearn to be again as unaware as a baby. Tonight, though, I am content with myself; I have found shelter for my family.

Our journey takes seven or eight days. The sun shines, rains fall, the sea rolls us about, the nights are raw with cold, but we are not tourists. We endure. One thing is especially difficult. The food we packed so carefully smells and tastes of gasoline. Whatever possessed us to carry fuel for cooking? Even a small spill of gasoline spreads and spreads. We spit out our precious raisins. Only small bits of cracker bread stay down.

Our ship makes one stop, about halfway to Beirut, at the island of Cyprus. There God finally smiles on us. We have an aunt who lives on the island. I have no idea how my mother gets word to her, but suddenly there she is on the dock, like a genie out of a bottle, carrying a huge basket of fresh fruit for us!

Pleasures can be measured only against deprivation and pain. The burst of flavor as the teeth break the skin of a purple grape, the ripe flesh of a fresh apricot against the tongue—what can compare, after four days of nausea and hunger? A basket of fruit. A miracle of the senses.

A few days later the sun shines on the slopes of Beirut as we ease into port. The squalid huts of the refugees cluster on the hillsides. My mother squares her shoulders. Sixteen tired hands hoist an untidy pile of sacks and boxes.

Life begins again.

4
Zahleh

E AST of Beirut, in the narrow mountain range running from north to south, lies the valley town of Zahleh, later to become a luxurious retreat for wealthy Lebanese. But when we arrived in 1923 it was a muddy river town, enclosed on two sides by steep hills. The hills were mantled gloriously in grape orchards, but the small dirt-floored houses crowding the unpaved streets boasted no indoor plumbing or running water. The structures sheltered a multitude of Christian refugees, many of them Armenians, most of them hungry, and all of them clutching a fierce hope for a better future.

Zahleh was to be our home for eight months. As I now look back at this period, it seems like an old silent movie, crammed with characters in rapid motion, full of struggle, change, laughter, and discovery. It was an important year, because as I roll the film more slowly in my mind, I realize that this was the time when I discovered, above all—myself.

In Zahleh, I felt free, and I gloried in it. See, there I am, racing through a maze of broken stone walls and crumbling buildings. Those are Roman ruins, built centuries ago, now a great playground for us children. There I am

again, where the river spills over in a raging waterfall. Be
careful! I leap from rock to slippery rock, mocking the
timid. And again, see me darting among the gravestones
of an ancient cemetery—Heranoush Gartazoghian, a small
girl, but leading the pack, quick and daring.

I see an old school building, and myself again. What am
I doing at my desk? The book is open, yes, but my fingers
are busy at something else. I'm winding a stiff horsehair
around my pencil; I slide it off. It forms a tiny ring. It's
part of a series of rings, which I knot together, until,
surprise! It has, after days of surreptitious work, become a
necklace. A necklace with a purpose. The next day, at
recess, I approach our teacher.

"A gift for you, my teacher!" I am all smiles. "To hold
your watch!"

He stares at my outstretched hand. "No, no! You foolish ungrateful child. School is for learning, not for hob-
bies! Be gone! Get to your books!"

I shrivel. A stab to the heart. But I recover. Very well
then, I keep my head bent to the books, my hand concentrating on the slow labor of lettering. I run home that day,
a tomboy as usual, but I make a decision not to tell my
mother about the horsehair necklace.

My energy seems limitless. I don't know why, because
none of us ever has a full stomach. Once in a while we
hear of visiting officials with truckloads of food and clothing, sometimes from Near East Relief, sometimes from the
Red Cross. But they never come to us. Everyone scratches
for work—odd jobs, anything; even Nazeli and her family
are now poor like us.

I am a girl-woman these days. Sometimes I play silly
games with Norayr, like the day someone gives us a drink
called tea. We have never tasted it before; it's delicious,
and we want to make it last as long as possible. When we

are down to the level of the last few centimeters, we break
cracker bread into our glasses. The tea absorbs the solid
and creeps up the sides of our glasses.

"Look, Norayr! My glass is almost full again!"

"No! Mine is higher, higher!"

We giggle, stuffing more cracker break into our tea.
Weak tea and bread make up our only food that day, but it
is the game I remember and not so much the hunger.

At other times I feel like a woman. Today I race home
from school, because my mother and I have a new job
which I helped to get for both of us. A Protestant minister
has come to take up his duties at the church. When we
were asked at school if anyone wanted to take the job of
cleaning the church, my hand shot up. Today our new
assignment begins. I drop my books and we hurry on our
way. We work hard, silently—two women side by side.
We have brought a mop and pail, rags, and a stubby
broom.

"Heranoush, this water is dirty already—run and get
me fresh water!"

The church is on a steep hill, like every other building
that does not sit on the river banks. I hurry down to the
water. Quick! Dip! Fill! Hurry back! So many times!
Sweat glues my dress to my body. Pain knifes into my
shoulders, and my legs tremble on the last pull uphill. But
at the end of the afternoon the tiles glisten in the chancel
and the wooden pews gleam in the soft light of sunset.

One job piggybacks with another. Today mother and I
trudge even further up the side of the mountain. We have
been engaged to clean house for the minister's family.

"How far, *mayrig*?"

"Close now, just beyond those trees. You see?"

"But—it is a long way to fetch water, is it not?"

"Wait and see, just wait and see!"

Whew! Well, here we are. The minister's wife takes us through the two-story house and shows us two magical things. The first is a silver handle which you turn, and out comes a stream of clear, cold water! One such handle is found in the kitchen, another in the bathroom. The other marvel is also in the bathroom: a spotless white seat, set over a bowl of water. When you pull a hanging chain, a gurgling whirlpool of water whisks away everything in the bowl and fills it again with sparkling water.

The indoor plumbing is a constant source of delight and mystery, except for the day when the minister's mischievous son snatches my knitted hat and gleefully flushes it down the toilet bowl. I'm too late to stop him but I have his shoulder in a grip of steel as we confront his mother with "the crime."

His mother stares, glares; then, letting out her breath, she smiles.

"Well, I guess the first thing to do is to get you a new hat!"

Sure enough, she appears a few minutes later with a woolen beret for me. And I have learned something about myself; sometimes confrontation is called for, and I, Heranoush, will not shrink from it.

It is late spring, and I no longer team up with my mother. I have found my own after-school job. I work for a dentist. Quite blasé about technological miracles now, I pump the mechanism which turns his drill. Between customers I keep the office clean. The pay is tiny but the satisfaction great.

School goes on, too. It's funny, my schooling has been so sparse and interrupted that I don't even remember my grade level, but I do remember, with joy and pain, the end of that school year. Everyone is bent soberly over the books in preparation for the final examination next week.

We will all be gathered in one big classroom: a panel of
judges will ask us questions, and there will be a prize for
the one who gives the best answers.

"But mayrig, how can I go to the examination? So many
important people—did you know that my dentist will be a
judge, mayrig?" I am arguing with my mother, several
days later: "You know that I have no shoes! Only felt
slippers! I can't go without shoes!"

My mother hears the anguish in my voice. She says
nothing. I ignore my books that night and go to bed with
the taste of ashes in my mouth. I press my face fiercely
into the rough blanket, cutting off breath and tears.

But my mother, my wonderful mayrig; on the night
before the tests she walks into the house and, like a magi-
cian, produces a bulging paper bag. Silently, she shakes
out its contents. There, in a nest of tissue paper, sits a pair
of soft black leather ballerina slippers, dainty and beautiful.

"Oh, mayrig, thank you, thank you!" I cry, slipping
them on and dancing around the room like a leaf in the
wind.

"Stop whirling about, child, and eat your supper! We
must wash your hair and you must get a good sleep so you
can think well tomorrow!"

Her voice is harsh, but I know it is not from anger. How
did she do this for me? What sacrifice did it cost her, I
wonder, as I try to make my eyes close in sleep on that
night so long ago.

The next day, in the examination room, the questions fly
at us like hungry hornets, until my mind buzzes in return.
I do my best, but finally I am just hot and tired. When my
name is called I can't believe what they are saying.
Heranoush Gartazoghian, first prize? First prize!

When my name is called again, I float up the stairs in a

dream. My eyes are focused on my ballet slippers. One step, two, three, four. Stop. I shake myself into reality, raise my head high, and walk forward to receive my prize, a narrow black box with a gold-tooled border. Inside lies a slender dark fountain pen, held against the white satin lining by a narrow elastic. No one I know has ever owned, and many have never seen, a fountain pen!

Later, after Norayr and mother are in bed, I sit at the table, pen in hand. Its graceful tapered point shines in the moonlight coming in the window, and for a while I am hypnotized. But then my mind looks inward, at myself. In these few months I have become my own person. I feel something in me, a kind of power. What is it? My body is small, but I have the will to try anything; I can work hard, I can think. But it's more than that. I guess it's a kind of faith that there are answers to any problems, and I will look for answers. I go to bed feeling, for the first time in my life, a joy in being alive, and in knowing who I am.

5

The Trip to America

LATE summer. A frantic telegram from Dikranouhi signals the beginning of the greatest change in my thirteen years of life, a change that will wrench me forever from my mother and plunge me into adulthood, willy-nilly, ready or not.

"Send her immediately," the telegram begs. We all know she means me, Heranoush.

And so, once more, the hurried packing begins, under the shadows of farewells to come. I am thinking of the lonely trip among strangers to the United States. My mother is thinking, "How shall we pay for her passage? We spent Dikranouhi's money to get to Beirut."

In the end the velvet pouch of jewelry has to be sacrificed. Dikranouhi will get the help she needs to care for her two babies, but her gold necklaces will go to buy me passage on a ship to Greece, a train to Paris, and a place in the lowest class on an ocean liner to New York City.

"Now remember, *yavroos*, dear one," cautions my mother, "you keep your money in the little pockets I have sewn into your slip!" I am about to walk up the gangplank of the Greek ship. I know my mother's voice breaks because she is holding back tears, as she has so many times before. We look into each other's eyes. She understands that I embrace her in silence because I am too burdened with fear and loneliness to speak. Where is my joy and confidence of early summer? Gone—pouf! I'm a child again, in a dark tunnel, with no one's hand to hold.

"Hey!" my mother calls to an Armenian family huddled on the deck, "this is my daughter, my Heranoush; maybe you would watch out for her a little bit? Yes?"

I shoulder the worn burlap bag which holds everything I own and turn away. The ship slides out into the morning fog.

All day we cut through an uncaring sea until darkness drops on us as suddenly as the closing of a door. I have snatched a mat from a pile on the foredeck. My bones press individually into it, seeking a soft spot. No luck. I hunch upwards, push my backbone against my sack of clothes, wrap my arms around my knees, and rock. Faster, fiercer, as the tears make hot furrows down my face. The ship's engine growls and belches below, churning a ghostly pathway behind us toward Zahleh and Beirut.

Like a litany, the black thoughts slip through my fingers: I am headed for America, knowing neither the way nor one word of English, with a bundle of rags for clothes and a small cache of money sewn into my petticoat. What if I am robbed? What if I lose my money? What if the strange fever that hits my body without warning should keep me from entering America? If Dikranouhi never meets me in New York? If I get lost and wander forever, homeless? I sob. The lumpy bodies around me snore.

Then a small miracle happens in the sky. The clouds slip apart and a nearly round white moon bursts through, scattering diamonds along the sea wake, bathing the wooden deck in light and shadow. A cool breeze dries my tears. Far off to the east, under the ship's starboard rail, a cluster of lights appear. Could it be Cyprus? Or maybe Constantinople? No, silly, it's just an island. No matter, I'll pretend it's Constantinople, where my sister Haigouhi and little John live. How I wish I could steer this ship right to Constantinople and visit you, Haigouhi! The last time we saw you, you were living on nothing but scallions and tomatoes. Then I remember that my sister's husband is living somewhere in Greece, or so it is said. If I could find him for you, my dearest, beautiful sister, I would make him return and take care of you!

The moon burns brighter above us. Bodies roll over, voices murmur. Then a low humming starts, changing to a song with words. Amazing! I can't see where the voices are coming from, but I know the melody. It's an Armenian hymn; I know it from my orphan days. My heart relaxes; I hum along with the unseen group. You are an Armenian woman, I tell myself, smart, proud, and lucky! I push myself down on my mattress and, magically, I'm asleep.

The days crawl by. I shadow the Armenian-speaking passengers. After the last of my dried fruits and flat bread disappear into my stomach, there is always a tidbit offered to me, a handful of crunchy chick peas or a bite of sausage. The Mediterranean is kind to us, calm and warm.

Finally a huge shoulder of land looms to our west.

"Is it Greece? Is it Hellas?"

"No, no, not yet! It's the island of Crete!"

The bearded patriarch who has informed us spends much of the afternoon enchanting us with tales of the ancient Minoan civilization on Crete, of the Minotaurs, the mazes, the kings and their astrologists.

The next morning, in a misty dawn, our ship weaves its way past hundreds of islands into the tangle of sailing craft and merchant ships that shoulder each other in the busy harbor of Piraeus, the port of Athens. The next several hours alternate between the boredom of standing in the long lines leaving the ship and the anxiety of keeping track of the Armenian group ahead of me on the way to the train. My "tourist" view of Athens consists of a moving circle of about two meters in front of my eyes. Within that circle I can see, besides the bodies ahead, my precious sack of clothes and my own tired feet. I can smell the lemon trees and hear the drone of bees. My nose tells me that we are passing a restaurant where fish smells fight with cheese smells. Ah, we are stepping onto a wooden platform, and there is our train. I squeeze aboard and settle into a dark red velour seat. Good! Safe again, for a time.

Did we change trains in the city of Athens? My memory clouds over. But I know that later that afternoon I am on a roaring monster making its way northward, on the way to Paris. I'm jammed between two women on a stiff plush seat. The man and boy across from us have flipped their seat backwards so that they now face us. What a wonderful gadget! I wish I could go up and down the long car flipping every seat backwards, just to feel the smooth brass fittings slide into place.

I'm hugging my burlap satchel. My eyes peer out over it. The man across from me pulls a lemon from a sack beneath his feet, slices it in half neatly with a short sharp knife, pops a lump of sugar in his mouth, and squeezes the lemon juice between his teeth. My own mouth waters, but I try not to show it.

Now, as if on a signal, everyone on the train pulls something edible out of somewhere: chunks of crusty bread, apples, figs, or cheese. I have eaten all my cache of food, and I know I shouldn't buy any from the limited treasure hidden in my slip. But we will be riding this train until late tomorrow! After all, it is over two thousand kilometers to Paris. My stomach keeps telling me how empty it is, so when the train puffs to a stop at a small station at the foot of a mountain, and a Greek vendor darts through with a tray of pastries and coffee, I tell myself that only a fool lets her stomach shrivel like a dried raisin! I point to one of the pastries which looks like a *khadayif*, sweetened with honey and filled with walnuts, and hold out a few coins. He takes two, grins at me, and hurries on. The Armenian woman next to me offers me some cold tea in a little paper cup. My stomach blesses me for this indulgence!

And so we snake our way through the darkening skies and the Balkan hills. Soon each of us wriggles into some sort of sleep position. The rhythm of the rails joins with fantasies of my unknown future; they circle in my brain in a slow dance until I fall into a deep sleep.

By late the next afternoon we screech to a stop in a cavernous railroad station. This is Paris! We all hurry to shake ourselves loose from our cramped positions, grab our possessions, and pour out of the long coach. We are laughing, stumbling, and chattering, nervous with fear, for many of us are ignorant refugees, seeing Paris for the first time.

The noise of it! The confusion! Redcaps staggering under baggage, newsboys hawking, conductors intoning departures in their splendid uniforms. As I scurry along behind my group, I brush by silken legs wearing soft pointed leather shoes; I see striped trousers with grey spats below the cuffs, fringed skirts, gloved hands—and ladies' hats! Straw hats, felt hats, silk turbans, hats brimmed and unbrimmed, ribboned and bowed, gloriously colored; and under many hats the bobbed hair of the new woman of the twenties.

Someone in our familiar band leads us to a hotel not far from *la gare*, the railroad station. It was probably small and modest, but on that day it seemed magnificent to me. I spend a long time admiring every plumbing fixture and smoothing the cool white bed sheets with my hands. Later I watch the soft lights come on in a procession up the avenue beneath our windows.

Here I am, in Paris, the one foreign city even a Middle Eastern girl like me has heard of, with a whole day's wandering ahead of me tomorrow! Maybe I will see the Eiffel Tower, or the great cathedral—what is it called? Notre Dame. That's the extent of my information, except that I know, as women know these things, that the shops of Paris hold elegant garments that all the feminine world craves and admires.

Later in my life I learned that this was Paris at the height of her cultural mystique; that perhaps not far from where I slept were many of the world's artists—Hemingway, Stein, Fitzgerald, Dos Passos, Picasso, Diaghilev, Monet, and countless others. Would I have felt less a stranger had I known that my sister Haigouhi, reunited with her husband, would soon be traveling to a new home in Lyons, where she would bear a second son, with the appropriately French name of Marcel?

Of course I know none of these things, but my one day in Paris remains a shining jewel in my memory for another reason entirely. I did something in Paris so unlike me, so foolhardy, that even now I can't explain it. Still, I have never regretted it, either.

Picture this: it is a soft Paris morning and I am scurrying like a frightened rabbit after a group of women from our hotel. In the distance we have spotted the giant black spider web which they say is the Eiffel Tower, but the glittering shops along the avenue are much more seductive. Too shy to invade the expensive boutiques, we finally march into a large department store. For the next two hours I am in a world so unreal, a world of such colors and textures and aromas, that I am bewitched.

How else can I explain what happens next? I have wandered into the hat department, when suddenly I see before my eyes A HAT. Not just any hat, this one is a delicate straw with a gracefully upcurving brim. Encircling it is a wide pink ribbon, ending in an elegantly pouffed bow, which perches like a nesting bird on the left side of the brim.

All the hungers within me, for love, for food, for security, focus on the hat. My body aches for it. It sits on a small pedestal on a glass-topped table. Sinking onto the upholstered stool in front of the table, I reach for it, place it, in slow motion, on my mop of curls, and the girl looking back at me from the mirror is, incredibly, a Parisienne!

Sanity melts from my mind. The salesgirl, who has been hovering suspiciously close by, relaxes her face into a smile as I delve into my secret pocket and pull out my money. I block out of my consciousness all guilt over the sacrifices this money represents and the knowledge that I may need it desperately before the end of my odyssey. As the salesgirl gives me back, thank God, some bills in return, I think: I am a poor refugee who has rarely known a day without hunger or fear, but I own a Paris hat, and I will love it forever!

The next morning sees us crowded onto a noisy train which hustles us to Le Havre, our port of embarkation. Le Havre is a port full of great liners that loom like floating buildings, a port where stevedores sweat and sailors swagger, where everyone and everything makes its own kind of noise. Somehow we locate our designated ship, the *USS Chicago*.

Hours later I am finally deposited, satchel and Paris hat intact, in a cavernous hall in the belly of the ship. On our descent to this level we have seen the glittering chandeliers, the tapestried walls, and the carpeted floors of First and Second Class. Our area is in Third Class. There are hammocks in tiers along the walls, some mattresses on the floors, and white enameled tables and benches at the far end. I feel very small in my corner. As the great ship shakes and growls beneath us, and whistles scream above us, I forget the excitement of Paris and the thrill of my purchase. All my mind sees is an endless, bleak ocean, on which I am a tiny speck bobbing about, floating further and further away from mayrig and Norayr, from my people and my language, from any of the homes I have known. I put my head on my arms and try to squeeze back the hot tears.

Something is hammering on my head! Stop that! And please, can someone put an end to this rolling and pitching about? Why are we moving, moving? Let me be still. Someone gasps and chokes beside me; a sour warm smell forces my eyes open. The old woman on the mat next to mine is sick again. I want to help you, old woman, but I can't. I too am sick. I can't even stand up.

How long has this ship been lurching through the waves? I haven't seen the ocean. I haven't eaten. How many times have I stumbled to the toilet and hung over the bowl, embarrassed and miserable? Will I die in this dark place? I don't think I care.

"Heranoush, here! A little water! Sit up a little ..." I recognize the woman bending over me by her head scarf and her smile. She is the one who never seems to be sick, even in the crashing storm we endured yesterday, when even the ship seemed to be in agony. She forces a few drops of water between my lips.

"Hey," she shouts to a tall man, "come over here, Johnny! Look at this little girl here, she must get some fresh air so she can eat—see how skinny she is, poor thing. Come on, help me get her out on deck."

I feel myself lifted. No, no, leave me alone! I must guard my satchel and my hat, please! But I'm too weak to protest out loud. Before I know it, I'm outside on the deck, bundled in a blanket against the wall, blinking in the cold sunlight.

Out here it's still noisy, but it's a different kind of noise from the constant thunder of the ship's engines. Here people shout, children run, and somewhere nearby guitars pick out rhythms and mandolins tinkle. Feet tap in response. Then right in front of me half a dozen young bodies leap up, join hands, and dance, laughing as they try to keep their balance on the slippery deck.

I'm surprised that the deck is so crowded. Who are all those people standing at the sides, watching and clapping? They are not all poor, not all long-haired women in babushkas or men wearing suits shiny with age. I see brocaded coats, gloves, carefully coiffed hair, and gold watch fobs. And I notice now that we have an audience leaning over the decks above, too, shouting encouragement to the dancers. There is a well-dressed woman standing near me now, muffled in a blue woolen coat. A young boy, her son perhaps, is with her. Suddenly her eyes meet mine and stop. Her face is so friendly and her smile so warm, I wish I could speak to her.

I've been helped out on deck several times now. There's almost no wind today, so I feel a little warmer. The dancers are swinging about madly. But I think my body is giving up; I guess this terrible seasickness is finding nothing in my insides to fight it off. The woman and the boy are there again, but I can't smile; I just want to sleep.

"Listen to me, child, are you Armenian?" The familiar language cuts through the haze. The woman with the friendly face is kneeling beside me. "You don't feel well at all, do you, little one?"

Her voice goes on, soothing and sweet. The rest of that day is vague. I can't tell you how it all comes about, but that night I find myself, magically, out of the squalor of Third Class and up in the Second Class cabin of my new protector and her son. I check quickly; my sack of belongings and my Paris hat are safe on a shelf. The cabin is a snug room, with three single beds and—wonder of wonders—its own bathroom! Hot water any time you want it! And a shower, the first one I have ever seen. The lady helps me step under the cleansing spray; when I am through she wraps a big towel around my skinny frame. Then she encourages me to take a cup of soup into my hands.

"Just sip it slowly, a tiny bit at a time. That's right. There now, Heranoush, we'll get you better in no time!" How does she know my name? Why is she doing this for me? Never mind. I'm here; the soup stays down; all the noise seems muted now and the ship's motion steadier. Day by day I am able to eat more; my stomach is settling down into its accustomed place instead of rising into my throat.

I love this cabin, especially the bathroom. I have washed every piece of clothing I own in the gleaming porcelain sink. Every morning I step into the shower and let the warm salty water slide down over my skin. Thank you, thank you, kind lady, my rescuer, whom I will never forget. I could not tell you now the name of that woman, but I can still feel the warmth of her caring, like a shawl around my shoulders.

I have lost count of the days, but today everyone is

talking about New York and when we will arrive.

"It will probably be midday tomorrow," says my protector. "And, Heranoush, I think I must tell you something."

I listen attentively.

"New York is the most exciting city in the world, but it is also sophisticated and cruel. We must not let you face it in the rags of a refugee."

As she speaks she is taking a dress from a box and underwear and stockings from a bureau drawer.

"Here now, my child, put these on and let me see if you are ready for New York!"

It takes me about two minutes to shed my old clothes and stand before the mirror in my new, white dress. Is it linen? Or a silky cotton? It feels soft and clean. And it's only a little bit too big. Where did she get it?

She stands smiling behind me in the mirror. "It's not a bad fit, is it, Heranoush? Now get your Paris hat and let's see our proper New Yorker!"

I snatch my hat and push it down over my curls. A new Heranoush smiles back at me. I turn to my friend. We both laugh, while our eyes fill up with tears.

Early on the last morning I make my way down again into Third Class, old clothes bundled in one arm, straw hat in the other. Lining up along the rail with the others, I hear a voice in my head which says, "Heranoush, why do you hang on to your old clothes? You won't ever need them again. Give them to the ocean!" So in the next moment, in a grand gesture of farewell, I heave my castoffs into the dancing waters far below.

Then my heart stops. I realize what I have done. There, in the brown bundle already disappearing in the waves, is all the rest of my tiny fortune, tucked away in my discarded slip! Foolish, impulsive Heranoush!

What can I do? Well, the first thing I must do is to pull my eyes away from the tragedy below. Then I must lift my head and look today in the face. I can join the hundreds of others, from so many different countries, who are now straining for their first glimpse of Lady Liberty and the tall buildings of New York.

Within sight of the skyline and the statue, however, our ship slows, bends to port, and eases up to the quarantine dock at Ellis Island. All of us from Third Class are marched ashore and into the building; there within its sterile walls we spend the night and wait anxiously for a morning of processing.

"Just say 'yes' to everything" is the popular advice. My line creeps up slowly, slowly, until I stand before the questioner, who speaks Armenian, thank goodness. Yes, yes, I say, over and over. Then comes the dreaded test by the eye doctor. If you have glaucoma, that is the end for you. Back you go, without ever having set foot on the mainland. What is glaucoma? Do I have it? But the doctor passes me with a quick nod—I am safe!

We successful ones file back on the *Chicago*, which is waiting at the dock. Soon we steam majestically up the Hudson River, slowly, much too slowly for our leaping spirits. The skyline of the city slips by, so tall and bewildering that my soul shrinks under its power. When we finally nudge up to the pier, I stare desperately down into the crowd of waving, calling figures on the dock. She must be there, my sister Dikranouhi! But where?

My eyes sweep the crowd like the lens of a camera. Suddenly, there she is. I *know* it's Dikranouhi; beside her stands her husband, with a little girl in his arms. That must be Ann, and the new baby, Zabelle, must be at home with a babysitter. I can even see the teddy bear Ann hugs to her body. Why can't they see me? I'm waving my arms off! I'm here, I'm Heranoush, your sister, all the way from Beirut!

Later, when I scramble down the gangplank and run into their arms, they recognize me.

"Oh, yavroos, yavroos," my sister laughs, holding me very close, "your hair! It's dark now, and short, and I remember you with long golden hair. That's why I didn't know you!"

We trot along through the city streets, arm in arm, shouting at each other happily in Armenian. The clatter and rumble of the traffic, the bodies jostling past us, the strange faces—none of this bothers me. I have been in cities before. But I am not prepared for what happens next.

We climb high up on iron steps onto a wooden platform, and then into a train. But this is not like any train I have been on before. This is a jolting, swaying monster which rockets through the air above the city on such narrow rails that you cannot see or feel the support. We will fall and crash, I know we will! But my sister and her husband only laugh at me. Even Ann and her teddy bear seem to enjoy this crazy ride. Later I, too, will become a placid rider on the Third Avenue Elevated, but on this day I grip the metal edge of my seat with all my strength.

An hour, perhaps more, passes before the sky train disgorges us from its jaws. We are in the Bronx now, Dikranouhi announces. Up a broad avenue we trudge, and at last we walk up the steps of the house where I will live for the next five years, while I learn what it means to become "an American."

6
New York

MY sister's house becomes a cocoon for me. When-
ever I run up the steps, the harsh foreign sounds of
English retreat from my ears, and the soft Armenian words
flow in. The smells of the kitchen—the oil, the spices, the
steaming pilaf—relax my stomach. And I know I'm
needed here. Life is not easy for Dikranouhi. She waits on
her husband, anticipating his needs, subduing the children
as well as she can. And her hands! So red and raw from
her allergy! So ugly that I cry for her. One look and you
know those hands should never be in dishwater.

"I'm here now, Dikranouhi." I jump up from the table
and hurry the dishes into the sink. "You won't have to
wash dishes or do the diapers or bathe the babies, or even
cook. Did you know I can cook?" I brag shamelessly.

My sister's eyes smile at me. She picks up baby Zabelle
and prepares to nurse her, while Ann toddles over to me
and hangs onto my skirt as I attack the pots and pans.

Work I understand, no problem. But school, in America, is a humiliation that is hard to take. At first it's not so
bad, because I start in the "foreign" classes. These are
schoolrooms where immigrants from any country can
meet the English language head-on. All nationalities

mingle, some of them bubbling with energy and dreams, some too shy or too exhausted to speak. But at least we struggle on an equal footing. The frowning Italian man next to me is trying so hard to count in English that his red bandana is choking him. The pale Russian girl, in a brown skirt to her ankles, peers out, tongue-tied, from under her babushka. We all repeat like a chorus whatever the teacher says: "Hello." "I live in New York." "My name is . . ." I'm catching on fast. Too fast, I guess, because in six months they tell me I am assigned to public school, with American children.

"But Dikranouhi!" I plead, "I have to go into the third grade! They will laugh at me, a big stupid thirteen-year-old!"

"No, no, child, they will like you and help you. Now go, and put a smile on your face!"

So I go, in my dress that droops to my ankles, but my sister is wrong. When I even say my name in that classroom they laugh, and I am so slow in writing my papers that even the teacher taps her foot and scowls. Thank goodness I sit way back in the last row.

"You'll see!" I say to myself with my teeth clamped tight. "You'll see!"

Every day I rush home from school, do the babies' wash, and then help with dinner. Actually, I like working in the kitchen. During this first year in America I become fascinated with foods. And why not? Dikranouhi's kitchen smells deliciously of spices, herbs, meats, and vegetables. You need something? There is an Armenian market right down the block. Imagine that? I love markets. I taste, smell, and touch everything I can, especially new foods. Bananas, for instance, seem exotic, but they call them fruits. They peel so easily, and inside they are like a dessert—not too sweet, not sticky, just right. I forget loneliness and embarrassments when I experiment with food.

Let me tell you of one wonderful help I have found in learning to cook. Once a month or so we ride the El to Manhattan, get off at 27th Street, and go to the famous Balkan Restaurant, America's first gourmet Armenian restaurant. A cousin named Nazeli is married to the owner, Missak Cholakian; so we are not only welcome as guests, but I can "hang out" in back, in the huge kitchen, a paradise of fragrant smells, shining utensils, and constant motion. I lean close and question, question, until someone laughingly pushes me away.

Meanwhile, I'm catching on at school. A small triumph: by midyear I advance proudly to the fourth grade. By fall, I'm in the fifth grade; by the next spring I'm sitting in the sixth grade. Not bad, eh? But I'll tell you, those sixth graders are still babies to me. I think I have lived twice as long as most of them. I feel like a woman. I yearn for a job, for independence, for money of my own—not only for myself but to send a little to my mother and Norayr.

"All right then, Heranoush," my sister smiles, "we know the manager of a factory where the Oriental carpets come in and are processed for sale here. We could get you a job there. But the work isn't easy. And of course you will still live with us—"

"Of course, of course. Oh, thank you, Dikranouhi—"

"Wait, hold on, there's something else to think about. You will have to go on in school, too. There are night classes you can attend. You must promise that you will go to them, at least until you are sixteen."

It's easy to promise because I do love to learn. Also, the idea of going out at night, to school, is exciting.

My job in the rug plant, however, is anything but exciting. It's a dark, joyless place, on 125th Street in Harlem.

All day long I hunch over the table where the rugs are spread. Over my head hang many narrow tubes, each ending in a pen which dispenses a color dye. These are rugs which have imperfections, perhaps where salt water has seeped in during the overseas trip, or where friction or sun has affected the colors. We "touch-up" workers color in the spots and restore the carpets to their original beauty. My back is paralyzed, my fingers sore and stained, by the end of the day.

No one molests me, but I am nervous among these strange faces, young and old, who toil beside me and walk beside me in the streets of Harlem. Also, I am having a hard time getting over my fear of the long ride on the Third Avenue El. You're being silly, Heranoush, I argue with myself; think of the dragons you have slain already!

Perhaps it was only my compulsion to move on, my restless urge to get on with the next thing, whatever it might be, but I changed jobs so rapidly in the following two years that I'm not sure I can remember them all, or the order in which I captured each one.

I remember getting a job in a training program of some sort. Mainly we sit all day monogramming initials on napkins, tablecloths, towels, or sometimes handkerchiefs. Not much of a challenge to someone who learned to make intricate Armenian lace in the orphanage in Constantinople. Most of the employees relieve the boredom by drinking cup after cup of Turkish coffee. I don't think my destiny lies in a never-ending pile of linens.

My next job, I think, is on the assembly line of the National Biscuit Company, down on the New York waterfront. Usually the machines thunder in here, but on one late spring day, May 20, 1927, our conveyor belt is silent. I'm leaning out the third-floor window, holding fast to my share of the sill, as thousands of other New Yorkers are doing on this day. We are all straining our eyes to sight a small plane passing across our field of vision from its take-off point at Roosevelt Field. The plane is headed for Paris. The lone pilot is Charles A. Lindbergh.

"There it is! I see it—there!"

We all stare silently. Will one of us make her dream come true some day? I don't even have a dream, only a will to survive. But seeing that plane and thinking about this Charles Lindbergh—it makes a difference to me. It marks the day when I feel truly like an American.

Meantime, however, I am becoming a woman, physically and emotionally. In spite of the after-work jobs I still do for Dikranouhi (who now has a third baby, Zaven), I draw upon energy as if it is a faucet I can turn on at will. I have discovered friends. We visit each other, we devour American magazines, we listen to records, we window shop. Occasionally, properly chaperoned, we even get to the movies. But of all the enticements America offers, nothing inflames my imagination like dancing. It spells romance, and freedom! When I pirouette in front of the mirror in my bedroom, my body seems as light as a cloud. How must it feel to be held in the arms of a man and circle endlessly to the beat of the music? My night-school classes, once a first priority, are beginning to give way to making friends and "growing up."

Just before Christmas, a lucky break gave me an unexpected boost up the job ladder. I spotted an ad in the paper for "temporary Christmas help" in Bloomingdale's Department Store.

Dozens of hopefuls line up at the application desk at Bloomingdale's. I should leave! But everyone will stare at me! I'll stay.

Finally the clerk hands me a form to fill out. "NAME:" it says. I giggle nervously. What employer, I ask myself, is going to decipher "Heranoush Gartazoghian"? Now is the time to make a change. Let me see: "Hannah" is close to "Heranoush," and "Gartazoghian" means "one who reads."

So, in a stroke of my pen, I become Hannah Reader, and I get the job! Fortunately, the temporary workers for the Christmas holidays are not expected to be veteran sales-girls, so I survive. And I love the chaos and intensity of the marketplace!

The most wonderful thing, however, is that now I have worked in an American department store. With that all-important reference I am able, soon afterwards, to land a position in the legendary Gimbel's, one of New York's largest department stores! My lofty status? I'm a clerk, in the basement, in the department of MEN'S UNDERWEAR!

So here I am, a brash, rash Armenian immigrant, on my first day, facing an array of order slips and rules that con-stitute an entire new language. A forest of symbols, codes, and procedures! Thank God there are sympathetic co-workers who rescue me many times during my learning days. Somehow I keep cool, until at last I *am* cool and confident. Maybe I'm a bit proud, too, at home and among my friends. To work at Gimbel's! Why, it is, among my immigrant peers, like becoming a college pro-fessor!

7
George

THE next year, when I turned eighteen, I had spent five years in the Bronx. New York was my world and I felt comfortable in it. But fate had set me from the beginning in a pattern of change and challenge, so I should not have been too surprised when something wonderful, yet disturbing, took me down a quite different path.

It's a Sunday morning and I've just returned from taking the children to Sunday School, as usual.

Dikranouhi calls to me as I'm taking off my coat. "Oh, Heranoush, would you mind running across the street to ask if we can borrow the iron?"

A married cousin named Margaret lives on the other side of the street. We borrow back and forth regularly. I'm glad to go over there. I love Margaret and her good-natured husband Hadji. Their house is relaxed and friendly.

I bounce in the front door. There, under a blanket, lies my cousin's husband (or so I thought), sound asleep on the couch.

"Wake up, you lazy bum!" I laugh, yanking the blanket off the motionless body.

Then I gasp. Not only is it a stranger's body, apparently

naked, but a stranger's eyes are staring up at me, bewildered but totally unembarrassed.

In a split second I'm crouched in an armchair, with my entire head buried in a newspaper. Oh Lord! He's young, and strong. I did see that much. What is he thinking? What is he *doing*? I realize that he is calmly getting dressed! What a cool one he is! Doesn't he know I'm still here?

"Well, you could tell me who you are, now that you've got me out of bed!"

My newspaper inches down as far as my nose. He is slim, dark—and Armenian, I think. I like his eyes, even though they are definitely laughing at me.

"I—I thought you were Hadji," I stammer. "I just came over to borrow—oh, my name is Heranoush Gartazoghian, but in America I call myself Hannah Reader— and Margaret is my cousin—." I stand up, take a deep breath, and look straight into those bold eyes. "Maybe you should tell me who *you* are?"

"I'm George Kalajian, from Cambridge, Massachusetts. Your cousin's husband is my brother. Okay?"

"Okay," I smile. Then I blurt out, "Can you dance?" I'm overwhelmed by my own forwardness.

"Of course!" he says, leaping up and spinning me around the room. The only trouble was that he fell all over his own feet, and mine, too.

"You—you have no idea how to dance!" I explode.

But he just laughs and keeps his arm around my waist until I twist myself free and run into the kitchen to find my cousin and the iron I had started out to borrow.

Surprise! I had not seen the end of George Kalajian. He and his brother Hadji hastily cooked up a scheme that afternoon to outwit the traditional sanctions against an Armenian girl going out with a stranger unchaperoned!

The plan worked perfectly. It went like this:

At 6 PM Hadji stands on the sidewalk under our parlor windows.

"Dikranouhi!" he yells.

She appears in the window. "What's the matter?"

"I owe Hannah a trip to the movies, because she beat me at the card game the other night. Would you ask her if she wants to go tonight?"

Dikranouhi reappears in a moment. "Okay, Hadji, she says she would love to go!"

7 PM. A figure waits in the dark at the foot of the steps. I hurry down to meet him. Only it's not Hadji at all. It's George Kalajian! What shall I do? He takes my arm, my resistance fades, and off we go.

George took me home from the movie in a taxi. I am reveling in the luxury of the transportation when he proceeds to wrap his arms around me and attempts to kiss me, right in the back seat of that cab! As if we had known each other for months! Who does this guy from Cambridge think he is? Anyhow, that's it for you, mister, I promise myself. I will never date you again.

But George doesn't go back to his job in Cambridge. Instead he courts me, with amazing energy, all through the next week. His good humor and self-confidence weave a spell over me. I find that I can talk to him so naturally that I feel as if I've known him forever. We laugh at nothing, at everything.

In the quiet times when we just sit and hold hands, I begin to learn about this man's fascinating past. He is a refugee from Turkey, from Evereg, where my own parents grew up. His story unfolds like the "Thousand and One Nights," but more of that later. For now, let me tell you how our romantic madness progressed.

At the end of the week, another surprise. George's older

sister, Zabelle, arrives all the way from Cambridge, to find out what is going on. I guess she makes a quick assessment of the situation and decides she approves of his whirlwind choice, because the next thing I know he and Zabelle head downtown to Tiffany's jewelry store—yes, *the* Tiffany's!—and, putting together George's last paycheck and all the other cash they have, they buy a solitaire diamond ring. I found out later that it was literally his last paycheck because he lost his job when he failed to return to Cambridge.

"For you, dearest one," he whispers that night, opening the box, where the jewel floats in luminous splendor against the white satin lining. "For you, and I'm not going back to Massachusetts until you consent to marry me!"

How can you resist such a man? I am eighteen, ready for laughter, soft words; ready for love. This man is rash, impulsive, cocky, but also strong, ambitious, and charming. So, do you believe it, at the end of that crazy ten days, I have said "yes" to George Kalajian! What awaits you now, Hannah Reader?

8
George's Story

GEORGE managed to get back to visit me often in the next few months. Sometimes on these visits, like the Arabian princess Scheherazade, he would spin tales of his incredible adventures before coming to America, leaving me in suspense from one episode to the next. It started like this:

George's troubles began in 1909, soon after a group of "liberators" took over leadership of the Turkish government from Sultan Abdul Hamid. Armenians rejoiced. The constitution would be restored; the massacres of the nineteenth century would never be repeated. But the new rulers turned out to be more butchers than saviors. The city of Adana, in southern Turkey, became the first victim. Rampaging soldiers killed, raped, and burned. Once again thousands of refugees crowded the roads, the churches, and the orphanages, as the new bloodbath spread through all of Cilicia and beyond.

North of Adana, in Evereg, where the Kalajians lived, the Armenian population woke one morning to find a terrible edict posted: "In three days your homes will be padlocked. You must leave this country and go to Syria."

George was a boy of eight or nine then, the son of a

respected merchant. The family was comfortably well off. An older brother and a sister had gone to America. With this disaster hanging over them, George's father gathered the rest of them together: George's mother, George, his three brothers, and his younger sister. Carrying everything they could pack on their backs, they fled on foot, southward to Aleppo, Syria. At Aleppo they managed to get on a train to Damascus. But Damascus was overflowing with hopeless refugees; so they set out desperately for Arabia, about one hundred miles away.

"In the small towns of Arabia we became homeless beggars. We took what refuge we could in ruined buildings, against crumbling stone walls. We found that there were several Christian Arab communities nearby. My father and my brothers foraged our way back and forth among these. But one day my father became very sick. We knew he was dying; we had seen death strike in many terrible forms already in our sad journey." George's voice is steady as he holds me in his arms and tells me this, but his eyes are burning holes of grief.

"Before he died, he called me and my younger brother Mike to him. 'You will live,' he said to us. 'You will see the world, and you will have a happy ending.'"

"How could he have known? The two of us did survive, and we are happy now, but the years between were horrible, at first . . ."

The story becomes so grim that it overshadows my own trials. George's mother died a few days after his father. The children heaped stones over the bodies.

"Is this all we can do?" they cried. "Let us ask the village priest to say prayers."

But the priest demands payment. "Surely there is something of value you can give me." He peers at our tiny hoard of possessions. "What about that bag of salt?"

They surrender the salt. He mumbles the prayers, and then there is nothing to do but survive, if that is possible.

Life is precarious when you pick through garbage heaps and animal dung for food. George's older brother is the next to die, poisoned by rotted food. Now the guardian of two younger brothers and a baby sister, George decides to leave the stench and decay of the village streets. He marches his "family" out into the fields and deposits them on a small hillside. Whatever they see the cows or sheep eating, they too will eat.

But grass and weeds are hard on the human stomach, and one day the youngest boy comes back triumphantly from a secret trip to the village.

"Look! See what someone gave me! A whole pail of wheat pilaf! It's all right, I've eaten some already!" He rubs his tight belly, and soon rolls over into an exhausted sleep.

"I'm going to eat some of that!" announces Mike, George's next youngest brother.

"No," says George, pulling him back.

"But we can't live on grass! I'm hungry."

"Leave it for him. We are older and stronger." They both turn aside and try to sleep.

In the morning the little brother who has eaten so well is dead, "poisoned," the villagers said, "by pilaf cooked in a copper dish."

Weeks, or months, later (who can tell time any more?) George's little sister dies of starvation. Alone now, George and Mike, day after desperate day, eat grass, or pick through dung heaps for wheat kernels, until the skin stretches so taut over their bodies that you can count every rib.

In the years after I married George I must have heard this next part of his story a dozen times, but I still feel the chill and excitement of it. Our children, and the neighbors' children sometimes, would sit enthralled as George relived the next miraculous years.

"I was about twelve years old by now," he says. "My brother Mike and I were facing starvation. One day I realized that we couldn't go on like this any longer; so I headed for the wealthiest house in the village, where the sheik lived behind walls, with his brothers and their families. They had stables, horses, sheep, goats, and a barn overflowing with grain."

Fifteen wild dogs guard the sheik's property. George walks right through the gate and approaches the building where the women live. Immediately the snarling dogs attack, tearing into him and biting deep into his legs. But on the heels of the dogs a half-dozen dark-robed women rush out, rescue him, and take him into the house. Clucking with pity, they carefully lay a hair from the dogs on each wound, then a coin to combat the poison. Touching soft fingers to his skinny body, they bind his legs. Best of all, they hand him a pail of food.

George shouts joyously as he returns to the fields, to Mike. "We'll go back when this is gone! They'll give us more, Mike!"

So George becomes a daily visitor, offering his help in return for the food. The women put him to work making the dung patties the household uses for fuel. He quickly learns to help with the animals too.

One day *two* ragged boys instead of one edge into the sheik's compound. Once past the circling, suspicious dogs, George leads his brother into the women's kitchen.

"This is my brother, Mike. Can he work too?"

"Why not?" they laugh. "Four hands can make dung patties more quickly than two!"

Good fortune descended upon them after that like

spring rains. One day the sheik's brother, riding through the fields, recognized the two boys and offered them the shelter of the barn. For several months George and Mike slept in the barn, cleaned the stables, took food out to the men in the wheat and barley fields, and helped the women, until finally they were accepted as part of the family.

The boys began to learn Arabic, and Mohammedanism, and even attended the village school. George remembered the morning prayer the students recited: "Grace to God and to Mohammed."

The Arab men taught them how to use knives, clubs, and even guns to defend themselves. Life, even on a sheik's land, could be violent and cruel. The boys learned fast, did all the menial tasks that "greenhorns" are assigned, and protested only once.

George remembers the day of the protest vividly.

"We set out with the men to clear the fields for spring planting. Mike and I rode camels, which we preferred to the horses; they are faster, you know. Anyhow," he continued, "we pulled up beside a large stone well."

"You boys can be a big help to us today," said the Arabs. "We're going to clean out this well for the season."

The boys leaned over the wide stones and peered into the darkness. Instantly they scrambled back, holding their noses.

"Agh! What a terrible smell!"

The men laughed. They knew exactly what caused the stench. In the long winter months death often visited these dry, harsh lands. A beggar stops breathing, slumps to the ground; one man knifes another in a split-second argument; a robber chokes his victim in the blackness of night. One can easily dispose of the body if there's a well nearby. So every spring the bloated carcasses and accumulated rot float on the murky waters below.

The cleaning method was simple. They would tie ropes around the ankles of several workers, lower them head first into the hole, then haul them up when they had gotten a grip on a body. George and Mike had no doubts about which workers would be chosen today.

"But—but—we can't swim!"

"Don't swim. Just hold your breath and feel!"

Neither brother dared protest further, but they could never forget the dark terror, the gagging and gasping for breath, the slimy touch of a dead man's fingers.

"Oh, George—how terrible!" I interrupt, and move closer to him on the couch.

"You do what you have to do," George shrugs, "and you never show cowardice in front of your Arab coworkers."

Life among the women of the sheik's compound did not require such proof of courage, at least after the initial incident with the dogs. Even the night the women practiced their tattooing skills on George proved more interesting than painful. Arab women love decorating their bodies with intricate and artistic tattoos. On this night Mike looked on as the women etched a design on George's arm: a sword and star, and a cross to signify that he was born a Christian. As he tells me this, I finger the tattoo. It is a beautiful design.

The sheik was a wise and successful businessman. Periodically he sent great loads of grain and livestock to the larger markets, and invariably his representative returned with many bags of gold. The grandmother of the household, whom the boys loved from the beginning for her compassion and intelligence, was apparently the treasurer and record-keeper of the business. She trusted them to help her put the gold in tin cans and bury it in deep holes dug in the floor in carefully designated areas.

Thus five years pass. The two orphans have become like sons to the sheik, who has even blessed the betrothal of George to his pretty daughter Neduva.

But small shifts of fate can start an avalanche of change. One day as George sits in the village waiting for the tinsmiths to re-tin the sheik's household cooking pots, he notices that one of the tinsmiths has the Armenian letters HN tattooed on his arm.

"You are Armenian! I am too!"

The men are wary. This strange young man wears an Arab burnoose, yet claims to be Armenian. George quickly tells the how and why of his situation with the sheik.

". . . and my brother and I, we are the same as you, we are your friends! Believe me!"

"Then come with us. Live with your own kind . . ."

But how does one leave a family that has given you life, hope, and even a daughter in marriage? Of course one cannot. But a seed of homesickness had been planted.

In late summer of that same year, the sheik contracted with a Bedouin caravan to take a load of goods to Damascus for sale.

"We begged to go along," said George, "and finally got permission. Our 'uncle,' the sheik's brother, had gone on ahead and awaited the shipment in Damascus. When we arrived with the caravan, he told us we had better go back to the desert as soon as the goods were unloaded at the market. Perhaps he was afraid that the city offered too many temptations to young men like us!" George laughed. "But we got him to agree that we could stay and return home when he did. Then we set off to see Damascus."

On the alert for Armenians, the two brothers spotted an Armenian priest in a cobbler shop.

"Throw them out!" shouted the cobbler, "they're

imposters, they'll just get you in trouble!"

But the priest believed them, and when in the course of exchanging stories he found that the boys came from Evereg, where the priest also had been stationed, he insisted that they come home with him. There he persuaded them that they should try to unite with their own people. The next morning when they returned to the caravan, they told the sheik's brother of their desire.

"And can you imagine, Hannah, he understood and sympathized?" said George, shaking his head in wonder. "He gave us a bag of gold, wished us well, and promised that we would always be welcomed back to our adopted family."

"But what about your bride, Neduva?" I asked.

"Betrothals can be dissolved easily in Arabia; all it takes is a statement of the wish of the prospective groom. I was naturally sad to be leaving Neduva, but perhaps she didn't mind that much. After all," teased George, "she was very beautiful and had many suitors."

Before long, at the request of the priest, the boys found themselves telling their story to the archbishop of Damascus, who ordered suits of clothes for them and arranged for them to live at the Orphans Relief Home. There the photographer took their pictures and the barber sheared off their long, Arab-style hair.

"We felt like strangers in our own skins," said George. "And we were suddenly homesick for our Arab family. One day we just left the orphanage and started to walk home. But I guess fate stepped in again, because at the edge of the city that same priest met us and brought us back.

"Soon afterwards we got a letter from our older brother, who had gone to America years before. He had joined the Foreign Legion during the War and now was stationed in a

Syrian military camp. He had been searching for his family for years and had finally tracked us down to the orphanage."

"Yes," I interrupt at this point because the rest of the story couldn't compare in drama to what went before. "And you finally rendezvoused with your brother and recognized him because he had one finger missing since childhood. Then you and Mike went with him to Aleppo, Syria, where the French government had established a protectorate. There the Red Cross finally located you. They had a letter and some money for you, sent by your older sister in America. She wanted all three of you to come and live with her in America, which you did, and," I grinned at him, "do you know why fate arranged all that so carefully?"

"Tell me, my dearest Hannah," he says, although he knows the answer of course.

"So that your older brother could marry my cousin and I could come over here to borrow an iron and find you sleeping on the couch and capture you for my husband!"

9
Marriage

"I would like very much for Hannah to visit me in Cambridge," George propositions my sister one weekend, not long after our engagement.

"My brother Mike and I live with our sister Zabelle, you know," he reassures Dikranouhi and her husband, "so she would be well chaperoned. In fact, Zabelle is recovering from a severe illness and would appreciate having another woman around to help a bit."

I listen to this conversation as demurely as I can, thinking to myself, "It will take more than an ailing sister to protect me from the advances of a wild man like you, George Kalajian!"

But any change of scene excites me, so I say nothing out loud. Several weeks later I arrive in Cambridge. My few days' visit stretches out; I never do go back to my sister's house in the Bronx. I stay in Cambridge to help care for Zabelle until my wedding in the fall.

It saddens me to know how much Dikranouhi will miss me. I already miss her. She has been like a mother to me for so long. But her daughters Ann and Zabelle will soon become efficient helpers in my place.

Cambridge thrills me over and over. It offers quiet

walks by the Charles River, the fragrant gardens and ancient elms of Longfellow Park, and the ivy-covered walls of Harvard buildings. The screeching traffic and bustling markets of the Bronx fade to a foreign echo in the back of my mind.

The Cambridge days. A quiet time before I become a married woman. I remember scenes, like postcards.

One raw windy day in April, George and I are huddled on a Boston sidewalk, cheering the last muddy exhausted runners of the Boston marathon as they stagger across the finish line.

"New Englanders are nice, but they are crazy," I remark. "Why do they push themselves like that, when it's only the winner who gets any reward at all?"

"They're proving that they can stick to something and not give up," he answers. "I guess it's not a woman's kind of contest," he laughs, teasing me as he loves to do.

"Women could run this race, too, if they wanted to, and I'll bet they will some day!" I flash back at him, suddenly much more enthusiastic over the race.

"Oh, really?" he says, steering me out of the wind and into a soda shop for hot coffee.

I remember the times we walked through Harvard Yard. You can feel the greatness of learning in such a place. We heard several of the Babson lectures that year. I listened as hard as I could. Dr. Roger W. Babson was a fascinating speaker.

"America is a land where initiative is rewarded," he said. "Whoever can produce even a better shoelace can get rich in the United States." Those words burned into my brain and never left.

Yes, opportunities do crop up like mushrooms in America. Shortly before we are married that September, George and Mike seize one of those opportunities. They pool their savings, and George uses stocks as collateral, to buy an ice cream spa located in a downtown building in Waltham. Fifteen thousand dollars! Sure, that's a lot of money, and they'll have to come up with monthly rent for the space in the building, but the brothers are natural gamblers. They breathe confidence. Why not? They manage a Liggett soda fountain now. Experience pays off. The fact that it is 1929 means nothing to cocky young Americans that year, nor to seasoned speculators either.

Our marriage plans gather momentum along with the business dealings. George and Mike, now hot-shot entrepreneurs, are cooking up a wedding on a grand scale. (According to Armenian custom, the groom and his family are responsible for the wedding arrangements.) It will be a double ceremony: George and I, Mike and his sweetheart Victoria. Attendants for both brides, of course, plus four bridesmaids, four ushers, two small boys as ring bearers, and two flower girls.

"We've hired two floors of a building for the reception, Hannah, one for eating and one for dancing!" George leaps up and paces the floor. "And we must have a caterer. After all, there will be about five hundred guests!"

"Five hundred guests!" I interrupt. "George, you can't be serious?"

"But I am. We have a lot of friends, some of them important people. What would you say, darling, if I told you that the *Boston Herald* will be sending a reporter and a photographer?"

I look up at my husband-to-be, shake my head, and surrender. "Could I expect any less from the man who once planned to wed an Arabian princess?"

As he promised, the *Herald*'s man does appear at the reception, with the photographer striding behind him, laden with tripod and heavy camera.

The caterer turns out to be an efficient Armenian woman who surprises us all by serving American style: black waiters bearing endless trays of elegant sandwiches, tiny cakes, and exotic fruits. I think my uncles and my godfather, and maybe even my Irish bridesmaids from the apartment above us, would have relished a hearty dish of chicken and pilaf.

I look at the faded wedding pictures now and I wonder again at the fanfare that accompanied our marriage. There I am, so young and serious. My long lace-edged veil is draped over my head and gathered at the ears in sophisticated New York style. Then it sweeps down to the floor, ending in a circle of net and lace at my feet. My sister-in-law Victoria is beside me, looking serenely lovely. The wired net "crown" on her head adds height to her stature. Behind us our husbands stand tall in their rented tuxedos, looking as smug and happy as two budding capitalists should look.

Maybe our dual honeymoon, which turns into a fiasco, should have been a portent of the financial crash which was to follow, but it seemed only very funny and frustrating at the time.

We're heading for Cape Cod for a lovely country honeymoon, the four of us riding in splendor in the Cadillac George has borrowed from Victoria's accommodating boss. George, with his brand new driver's license tucked into his pocket, whistles a confident tune behind the steering wheel. We cross the bridge and delight in the cool sea air and bowered roads of Sandwich and Barnstable. Cape Cod is far from the Boston metropolis.

Suddenly, with no warning, BANG, CRASH, CRUNCH! George has veered off the road; plowed through sand, rocks, and bushes; *and* something very ominous has happened to the car we do not own. I can feel it.

George Kalajian, left, and
brother Missak (Mike)
Kalajian, on the day of their
double wedding,
September 4, 1929.

Hannah and George
Kalajian on their
wedding day.

Double wedding party. Hannah and George, center left, Victoria and Mike, center right.

"Everybody all right?" George's voice croaks.

We brides tumble out of our seats and try out our arms and legs.

"Okay, I guess," I say, "but look at the car! Oh, George!"

He gives me a quick hug and flashes me that cocky grin. A few minutes later he and Mike walk soberly up to us.

"Uh, look, it's a broken axle. We're not going anywhere tonight, girls."

Well, I must say those two guys are resourceful. They scout around and discover a small boarding house up a side street. It's called "The Willows." The proprietors take us in, make us comfortable, cheer us with hot food and strong British tea; and there we stay, marooned in Dennis on the Cape, while we wait for a new axle for the Cadillac to be trucked down from Boston.

We had expected to tour the Cape, from the bridge to quaint old Provincetown. But our hosts at "The Willows" have made us "family," and the quiet beauty of their garden and the pathway to the sea beyond are probably more romantic than anything we could have discovered.

"A lot safer, too," I tease the men, "than sitting in that car with you two cowboys driving us around!"

Well, when the axle arrives we have to head right back. No more dream time; the new business venture in Waltham demands immediate attention. We say good-bye to our kind hosts and drive, very carefully, north.

The four of us set up housekeeping together, in the same apartment, in Waltham. It's a great adventure for me, getting to know Victoria, buying furniture, cooking in my own kitchen at last, and working at the spa. We work in couples, alternating shifts, one couple taking mornings, the other taking afternoons and evenings. It's a good system, ensuring us companionship and privacy and enabling us to keep the store open seven days a week. A year of high energy and high hopes quickly passes.

On October 29, 1929, the financial heartbeat of the United States stopped, fluttered, and staggered on feebly. The nation's businesses began to slide. From 1929 to 1931 stockholders lost fifty billion dollars.

George and Mike worked valiantly against the rising tide of fear and pessimism. George's buoyant sense of humor carried all of us along, and there were some wild, wonderful, laughter-filled times to cherish. We were very young and of course we believed that nothing could diminish the golden glow of America the Beautiful.

But there never seemed to be enough customers. And when George's debts on his marginal stocks were called in, the laughter grew thin and work hours lengthened. Nothing worked. The business was failing. I watched my proud husband turn into a grim man who acquired a gun and talked of suicide.

Finally, in 1931, the man who had sold us the spa returned from his long wonderful vacation in "the old country," Italy, and took back our store for default of rent payments.

Perhaps the finality of being completely broke brought George out of his depression. We are sitting at the kitchen table, I remember. . . .

"It's going to be all right, dearest." George reaches across the table to hold my hand.

"We'll go back to New York, to the Bronx if you want, Hannah. You'll see your sister, we'll rent an apartment, and—" he pauses and grins, for the first time in weeks, "I promise never to sleep naked on the couch on a Sunday morning!"

I laugh then. How can I help it, remembering our first encounter? "You probably couldn't," I say, "because we may not have a couch!"

My idle words turned out to be true. We divided all our furniture; Victoria kept the living-room set and I chose to keep the dining-room set. I loved that set, the dark gleam of the mahogany, the elegance of family meals at that table. It gave me comfort and pride through many uncertain years. We didn't invest in a "proper" living-room set until more than thirty years later! So what? I didn't care. Isn't it true that it's love and food that create a home? We had both.

We do head back to New York in 1931, with our dining-room set, one bedroom set, and empty pockets. George tries several jobs, settling in on one in a produce market where he works six days a week for fifteen dollars. Fifteen dollars a week? In 1931 that's pretty good. What scares us is the apartment rent. Thirty-four dollars a month! More than half his income for a place to live! It means I must count out eight dollars from every week's wages and deposit it into an untouchable bank account. Somehow, too, I must put aside a dollar now and then to send in my letters to my mother. George's gambling days are over.

What a time to have a baby! But when our first child bursts into the troubled world of 1932, we welcome her with pure joy. We name her Cohar, "precious jewel," for my mother.

Cohar fills my days. Each night I recite her accomplishments.

"She looked straight at me today, George!"

"She knows your voice—look, George!"

"Write it down, for posterity," he teases.

Good idea! I skim off nickels here, pennies there, until I can buy a real "baby book." Then I record her development as carefully as any scientist in his lab.

George vows that his daughter will have the best, nothing less; so he foregoes the subway and walks the ten-mile round-trip to the market each day, on tired feet, so that she can take her first steps in Stride-Rite shoes.

He shrugs off the ominous weakness that overcomes him sometimes at work. He is grateful that the owner is kind. The man always slips an arm under George's shoulders and eases him down the back stairs to the cellar.

"Stretch out there on these boxes, George," he says. "Take a few minutes—you'll be okay. It's all right."

Each time George pulls himself together and hauls his body back to the fruit stands. You don't let yourself think ahead about these things, or look for causes. But a body nourished on grass and terror in childhood bears internal scars that never heal.

Cohar is a healthy three-year-old when we rejoice over the birth of our little son, Hagop, or Jack, as he quickly becomes. It's 1935. The homeless of New York City still queue up in soup lines, the radicals rant of Marx and Lenin from street corners, but Roosevelt's "New Deal" is taking hold, spawning jobs and hope in the marketplace.

Life is hard for us. So? It's worse for others. We are a family, and we don't go hungry. But a familiar restlessness possesses me. There is something better out there, better than mere survival. If I could just recognize it, touch it, find the way! Somewhere, sometime. When I can pause for breath.

10

Worcester, Massachusetts

GEORGE has been thinking, too. One weekend he releases a surprise. It's Sunday morning. That means there's a white tablecloth on our dining-room table and breakfast is more leisurely. The coffee is hot and strong, the *choereg* (Armenian sweet rolls) fresh from the oven.

"There are four of us now, Hannah," he begins.

"Is that news, George? I can see Jackie in his crib, and Cohar is eating her cereal beside you."

He laughs. "How would you like to pack up soon and leave New York?"

I set my coffee cup down and wait.

"You can't get anywhere in New York. It's too big. I have a friend who has opened a large grocery store, called the Star Market, in Worcester." (This market, an independent store, had no connection with a later chain of the same name.)

"Worcester?" I ask, shaking my head.

"It's an industrial city in Massachusetts, only about forty miles west of Boston."

George leans closer. "My friend needs someone to run the store for him. But I have to take the job right away! It sounds very good, Hannah!"

One more great opportunity? Out loud I say, "But the baby . . . and we can't just walk out of this apartment!"

Now that he knows I'll go, he is as fired up as when we first married.

"Look, no problem. I'll go ahead and find us a place in Worcester. We'll give a month's notice right away. Rents will be cheaper in Worcester; it's a big city but nothing like New York. You'll like it, Hannah. I have a good feeling about this!"

A little more than a month later, I take the train to Worcester. Jackie sleeps on my shoulder or gurgles peacefully among the bags and bundles on the seat beside me, while Cohar presses her nose against the window and bombards me with questions about "Woo-sher." Little gypsy, she is happy to be on the move, to anywhere.

George scoops us up in a bear hug as we pick our way through cavernous Union Station in Worcester. He piles us into a Main Street bus and minutes later we are at "Lincoln Square."

"Right over here now, we have to get across those railroad tracks, come on," he urges, leading the parade. "But see! This is a beautiful part of the city. Over there on the left is the Armory, and turn around a minute, behind you is the Courthouse and the Auditorium."

On the other side of the tracks he goes on. "Up that hill in front of us is Memorial Hospital, on the right over there is our competition—Brockelman's Market. Don't worry about that, competition is good! Now look to your left. Up there, you can't see it, around the corner is the Star Market, *my* store, and can you see the big building across the street?" We're starting up Lincoln Street and he speaks. "That's the Sawyer Lumber Company."

The only thing I'm thinking is that in whatever direction I look in this city there is a hill. George says it's called "the city of seven hills," like Rome.

George is pulling us up a steep side street. "Look, Hannah, you see all these three-story houses? Worcester is famous for them. They call them 'three-deckers.' And here we are! Our apartment is in there."

He points to a narrow "three-decker," enclosed by a few feet of trampled grass. In the back I can see three layers of back porches where laundry flaps on identical circular clothes reels.

I'm sure George saw every occupant of every tenement around Lincoln Square as a potential customer for the Star Market. We lived on that hope for several years. The market did well, at first, but it became clearer every year that George's friend, the owner, was a rash, impetuous man who overspent and overinvested, until finally bankruptcy loomed closer and closer each month.

"Bankruptcy? Oh, George!" I can't keep the desperation from my eyes. No wonder, since I'm holding to my breast our third child, a daughter whom we have christened Carol. What now for all of us? What if the market closes?

The year is 1939. The shadow of the war in Europe hangs over us. A monster named Hitler has gobbled up half of Europe and some suspect he plans to purge Germany of the Jews. I know about purges and dictators. Somehow the five of us must survive whatever is ahead, but more than that, we must build up resources against the future.

"Don't worry, we'll be okay. I'll find something, there's more work around now."

George is talking to rebuild his own confidence. I find myself charging into his speech, with an aggressiveness unlike a good Armenian wife. But this thing must be said.

"George, no more of this working for someone else. You

must work for yourself. It's time we had our own store. We'll start looking for the right place, and we'll find it."

He stares at me. Then he nods his head and leaves the room without saying a word.

By the time the Star Market has closed, we have found "the right place." It's a double storefront at the bottom of Lincoln Street, with a barber shop on one side and a candy store and soda fountain on the other. Behind it, built into the steep hill, clings a two-family house. The candy store is for rent. Shall we give it a try? Deep breath. Yes. Done.

Maybe you can imagine how we scamble to set up our store. We mop the dark oiled floor, dig into corners, scrub wooden shelves, and climb to the ceiling with our suds. Do you remember the white-enameled metal tiles on store ceilings in the forties? Each tile stamped with a design? A challenge to clean. We work like frenzied elves.

George races to stock his market. Basic canned goods on the shelves. Bins for vegetables and fruits. Wire racks of soda bottles. A big noisy refrigerator bulges with milk bottles, egg cartons, butter, and cheese.

There's a wooden counter on one side. The cash register goes on the end by the door. Candy jars nearby. Tobacco and cigarettes behind, on the wall.

"And from here to the end," puffs George, pointing back along the counter, "we'll have our ice cream bar, very soon."

We are in business. Open early, stay open late. You expect that. Groceries sell best at the odd hours when Brockelman's, across the Square, is closed. But coffee and doughnut sales soar as the Sawyer Lumber workers discover us in the early mornings.

Baby Carol is about a year and a half when we get a chance to plunge again, for our future. The whole building, with both stores, along with the house behind it, is for sale!

How wonderful it would be to live practically on top of the store! No more trotting up and down that hill with baby on one hip, coffee pot on the other. No more rent to a landlord.

"How much, George? What are they asking?"

"No, how much would they settle for?" George has the gambler's gleam back in his eyes.

He bargains them down to $7,000. What shall we do? Yes, we'll take it.

It's a good move. Oh, the bills, the loans, and the payments press on us constantly. But it's for ourselves, isn't it? The rented "flat" on the second floor pays for ours on the first. Two small bedrooms. Well, we'll put beds in the living room for two of the kids. No living-room furniture anyway, so why not?

This whole double store to occupy! The pace becomes frantic. Scrub out the barber shop. What a terrible mess! But look, now we can have one side for an ice-cream bar, and the other for the market.

"We'll open this wall between!" George explodes with plans now. "And we'll install a completely modern soda fountain as soon as we can!"

More bills, more loans. The new arched walkway between the two stores creates a huge open look. But the thrill of our lives comes several years later with the installation of the new soda fountain. Old counters and shelves disappear; and in their place stands a gleaming expanse of polished chrome and steel! Electric hot plates for coffee. Stainless steel sinks. Push-button syrups. Cohar and Jackie try every stool and spigot, enthralled, while Carol tumbles about, laughing because everyone else is laughing.

Across the entire store front now, the world can read "George's Fruit Market and Luncheonette." Big square letters. You can see them from Main Street. Evening trade jumps, and noontime customers increase. Coffee and doughnuts expand to sandwiches and pies.

George has built a connection between the back door of the Ice Cream Bar and the cellar of our house. Because of the steep slope they are on exactly the same level. A dozen times a day I negotiate that flight of stairs and the passageway, shuttling baby, coffee, sandwich fillings, and pastries.

Gradually our family life gravitates to the store. We find it easier to eat our meals there. The electric hot plate always holds a steaming pot of pilaf or meat or soup for the children when they run in from school at noon. We eat in the booths Daddy has built along the wall.

"What's that wonderful smell, Hannah?" asks a man perched at the counter.

"It makes me hungry!"

"What is it?"

"Here," I say, "taste a little, it's rice pilaf . . ."

"M-m-m, you're a good cook, Hannah," they always say, no matter what hits their tongues.

Well, if it's that good, maybe I should make enough for my customers too! Before I know it the pot gets bigger and bigger. Daily specials, American style. I turn out baked beans, chop suey, beef stew, macaroni and cheese, whatever they like. Ah, but on Wednesdays I lure them from the American carbohydrate, potatoes. Wednesday's special is roast chicken and Armenian pilaf. The customers love it. More and more employees cross the street from the lumber yard, even William Sawyer, the president.

Sometimes I wonder at George. The man is an extremist. Downstairs at 7 AM and he seldom trudges upstairs until after 10 PM. Once in a while he allows himself a little nap after the noon rush. But is that enough? We are all tired, but he is wound too tightly, I'm afraid.

Maybe I should have listened more carefully to my premonitions, who knows? In 1942, when Carol is barely three years old, George collapses. It begins with pneumonia, but he is bedridden for two long years before he makes it down the stairs and into the store again. The era of wonder drugs lies ahead. We forget how long an illness could linger in those days.

What does one do in such a situation? The phrase "superwoman" had not been coined, and I would have scoffed at it. We had to go on. I didn't think, I just did what had to be done.

11

One Day at a Time

THOSE two years—1942 to 1944—what a nightmare. I get tired remembering. Sometimes I wonder how it affected my children. They all had to be part of the team.

Up at six. Out of bed, everyone! Clean clothes laid out in the kitchen. A white starched uniform for me; slide it on quickly.

"Downstairs, everyone! Cohar, watch Carol on the steps. Jackie, hurry down and get your wagon. Do you have your heavy jacket? It's freezing outside!"

Jackie has tears in his eyes. I know why. Early every morning he has to be waiting at Ryan's Bakery, on Main Street, to pick up fresh doughnuts. The pies and cakes I bake myself, late at night.

"Mama, I don't want to go. It's too cold. I don't feel good. The big boys always tease me . . ." Moist eyes plead with me. He's just seven years old.

"You will go. Now. And you will go tomorrow and every other day. So stop talking and move."

He goes. My heart goes with him. I worry about this journey he must negotiate each day, crossing the busy railroad tracks, through Lincoln Square where seven streets

intersect, dodging trucks, cars, and buses, then up Main
Street to the bakery across from the courthouse. Be careful, my little son.

Cohar is ten, a faithful helper. She watches over Carol
and sees that they both have breakfast while I run up to
check on George and start the cooking for later. Down
again. Cohar is serving the breakfast customers. She'll be
on duty at noon, and again after school, so that I can get
upstairs to attend her daddy without leaving the store
unattended as I must at other times.

Every Friday morning Cohar will set out for the fish
market at dawn. Friday means "chowder special" in our
lunchroom. Cohar selects the fish. Her judgment is as
good as mine. I concoct the chowder, with milk, the New
England way, even though my Near East psyche prevents
me from tasting such a mixture of dairy products with
animal or fish.

"Try it," coaxes Cohar. "You made it delicious!"

I look at her and think of myself at eight or nine, when I
would run to help my mother in the tobacco fields in our
village. The same story, in a way. A mother struggling to
survive, a daughter who must grow up too soon. But this
daughter—both these daughters of ours—will know that
they are cherished to the same degree as the son. This I
swear.

The day goes on. I fly from the grocery side to the
luncheonette side. I meet the delivery trucks, pay the
drivers, make out orders, pay bills, check the inventory,
call suppliers, and keep the shelves stacked. Jackie should
be able to help soon with the unloading and stacking.

The children eat supper in the store, while I pop Carol
into the tub and try to get something nourishing into
George. Then I slip into a clean uniform and wear a smile
behind the counter as the teenagers drift in for sodas, ice

cream, and candy. Gradually their bright chatter fades, and only an occasional customer stops in the darkness for bread or milk.

When I turn the door sign to "Closed," the clock reads 10:15. I'm anxious to get to my night work. Upstairs in the quiet apartment I start a wash, assemble ingredients for the next day's menu, sort the mail, mend clothes, and plug in the mangle. The mangle, a machine that draws dampened laundry items between hot padded rollers, is a blessing. For one thing I can sit. Everything slides quickly through its steaming cylinders. Tired as I am, I get satisfaction from layering up the clean starched clothes, one pile for the children, one for my uniforms, and then a stack of towels and linens.

This routine I can stand. One goes through the motions. But there are moments that break you.

I remember one morning. I must run up and get the pot roast which has been slow-cooking in the oven, because the lunch crowd will very soon push through the door.

"Hannah, is that you?"

George's voice reaches me as I hit the top step. He's restless, feeling better.

"Okay, okay, you want to sit by the window? There, that's good. I'll come up again after the lunch hour, all right?" A quick touch to his shoulders.

I race to the kitchen. Ouch, that pot is hot! And so heavy, with all that gravy and the vegetables. I can hardly get a grip on it. I kick the door open and start down the stairway. My arms ache already. I should put it down, but I'd better keep going.

Halfway down the stairway—catastrophe! One foot catches on the tread and the big pot flies from my hands. It clatters and bumps its way to the cement floor of the cellar. And on every step, steaming rivers of meat and gravy collect! Colorful useless vegetables rolling and sliding everywhere! I sink down in the mess, defeated, sobbing. No, it's not the end of the world. Food can be replaced. But something has given way deep inside me. A door bangs below me, voices and footsteps cross toward the lunch counter. I can't move from this spot. All the weary hours, all the struggles of my life, sit on my stomach and choke my spirit.

Of course I got up off those stairs. The customers ate. The stairs got scrubbed. I smiled over the ice cream tubs. But inside I carried a terrible exhaustion. I didn't know I was having a breakdown. I knew only that a captive demon gnawed at my insides but never quite escaped. My body paid dues to it over the next dozen years, with stomach trouble, bouts of illness, and operations.

12
Peaks and Valleys:
A Family Grows Up

GEORGE recovers as my body takes its downturn. He's back in the grocery store, making customers laugh, gaining new friends, and pushing himself again through fourteen-hour days. If frustration or uncertainty rub him raw, he eases his spirit his own way, late at night, when he lifts his whisky glass and lets the liquor slip cool and comforting along his throat.

World War II rages about us in the newspapers and comes closer as our evening hours bulge with teachers and students from the nearby Boys' Trade School, where night classes train men and women to work in munitions plants.

No matter how busy the supper hour, however, the last booth stays free each night, for the children to sit and do their homework.

"Go sit in the last booth! Take your books!" They laugh about it now, a family cliché, but it was then a sacred priority.

A priority not only for the children. Do they know how eagerly I, their mother, look forward to the homework hour in the late afternoon? It's the way I educate myself. Every book they bring home—science, poetry, geography—I read too. I can't devour enough of this world they carry in their satchels.

"So, what are we studying today?" I squeeze into "their" booth while George wields the ice cream scoop behind the counter.

"A new history book, Jack?"

"It's bor-i-ing, Mother!"

I'll snatch that "boring" book the minute you go to bed, son. "Read!" I direct him.

"Here, Mom, try my algebra problems!"

Cohar knows I'll take the bait and help her. Maybe she sees how the tiredness leaves my shoulders as we bend to the page together.

So our circumscribed world nurtures us as it holds us captive. The war ends, and the Great Depression lies buried with it. Business is steady. Now, now can we look beyond the store?

Our escape hatch turns out to be a camp on Thompson Pond, in Spencer. Not far from Worcester, but light years from "George's." A precious weekend retreat.

We build the camp in 1945. Cohar is sixteen this year, Jack is thirteen—old enough to help in the building, and Carol is a sweet nine-year-old. On Sundays the "Closed" sign hangs on the market door. The cottage is alive with teenagers, and Daddy often invites favored customers to join us. Come on, there's lots of room out here.

The camp spells freedom for them, a sweet release. For me, well, the cooking duties are prodigious at the lake, but how can I not be happy, looking at their faces? They will remember these days, as I hold in my heart the camel ride with my father, the outing in the park when I was an orphan, my Paris hat. I look at my family, my most precious gift, and I rejoice that every special day we've shared has been captured on film, in the home movies I've taken and carefully preserved.

Another satisfaction. We have taken over the second floor of our house in Worcester. No more renters. Four more good rooms! Out go the beds from the living room. With a little ingenuity and small slices from the budget, the children have spaces of their own. Personal choices and self-respect.

And a bedroom left over! My mind leaps across the ocean. My mother, now old and sick in Lebanon, will never make the journey to America. But Haigouhi's son Marcel would love to come to us. In 1954 Marcel becomes the first of a procession of relatives who occupy the empty room. How can you refuse, when you know how it is still for many of our people across the ocean? A little food, a little space. We have that much to share.

After Marcel comes Mari, a grandniece. Poor child, she is in need of a heart operation. Then my brother Norayr's son Ara. Our visitors blur in my mind. That's okay. One gives and one receives.

In 1955 Cohar, my first born, my "jewel," marries and moves to Connecticut. Her husband, Walter Bartlett, is not even an Armenian! So? This is America. When Cohar and Walter give us Debra, our first grandchild, I feel a weight of sadness lifting from my spirit. New life, new hope. Cohar brings Debbie to us as often as she can, though she teases us for crying with joy as we hang over her crib.

Jack is the next to go, in 1956. He and his beautiful Lorraine will head for California right after the wedding. California! When will I see my grandchildren?

"You're getting way ahead of yourself, Mother," says Jack, the usual irrepressible grin breaking over his face. "Besides, California is not really so far. You'll come and visit! Don't forget, Aunt Dikranouhi lives there now too, and many of our cousins! I can use my engineering training in California; they're crying for men like me!"

He's laughing at me, but he knows I'll bless his journey. We embrace, and they are gone. Back to the store. There is much to do, on any day.

13

The Birth of a Business

THE last problem we expected to face in the 1950s was another threat to our livelihood. It hit us about the time Cohar, and then Jack, got married. Bulldozers, steam shovels, and work crews rumbled into Lincoln Square. Day by day they cracked pavements and dug deep into the earth below. Businesses around the square buzzed with rumors.

"What's going on?"

"They're putting a bypass tunnel under the square! The railroad may go too . . ."

"Yeah, they say it'll take years to complete. What a mess this whole area will be!"

Rumors became truth. The Sawyer Lumber Company lost its site within the first year and moved three miles north. Our best customers!

"It's going to be okay, Hannah."

George and I are sitting in the last booth, grabbing a bowl of lamb stew while Carol takes care of the last of the lunch customers. I think he wants to talk about the construction outside, but I hold back a bit.

"I wonder how soon Carol will be leaving us too?" I say idly. We both turn to watch our seventeen-year-old scattering her charm the length of the lunch counter. Her black curls sit like a crown on her head. Her beautiful smile makes her everyone's darling. She's all woman, with her daddy's gift for making friends.

"Look, Hannah," George draws me back. "Let's talk. Sawyer's is moving only a couple of miles up the road. They'll be back to see us. And the Morgan Construction Company is still down there on the corner. We have other regulars too."

"Yes," I say, "but we still don't know whether the plans call for reconstructing us right out of our store!"

George says nothing. I sit there thinking. In a few years I'll be half a century old. I feel a frustration I can't push away—half emptiness and half puzzlement. It's as if I've been in a cocoon for a long time, waiting to shake myself free. This has been a period of marking time—for what? I dream of a solution to this endless parade of hours behind the lunch counter, but I always wake up to a body still bone tired and a mind too numb to plan.

The spark that revolutionizes my life ignites almost by accident. An enforced vacation in California follows several operations and one episode that convinced me I needed a long rest. I remember the hot afternoon when I was stubbornly pushing a lawn mower along the steep banking that sloped from our house to the store. One minute the grass is flying, the next I'm collapsed beside the mower, gasping for breath.

During the hospital stay afterward, when various doctors were shaking their heads over me, I finally gave in. I would go to California as soon as I could, for a complete separation from responsibilities.

"You'll love it," the family urged. "Besides, California is bursting with our relatives. You can bounce from one to the other! You'll see Jack and Laurie and your new grandson Jeffrey. Cousin Missak has moved "The Balkan" out there too."

I had to smile, remembering my teenage enchantment with the kitchen at "The Balkan" restaurant in New York.

"And, Mom, you'll see Aunt Dikranouhi and the children!"

That was true. My beloved sister had moved to California several years before. And half a dozen cousins had settled out there. The final argument: my nephew Zaven, visiting from California, would fly with me, so that I wouldn't have to make the trip alone.

California. There's a wildness and freedom in this California air. Maybe I'll catch some of it. Jack and Laurie seem very happy here. And my beautiful grandson feels wonderful in my arms. Jack has an important job, related to space satellites for NASA. I love to hear him talk of machines and designs. Energy can be catching. I hope so.

One day, on a visit to Cousin Missak's home, I get the first flash of what will be my personal revolution. At dinner there are, of course, steaming bowls of pilaf.

"I can't eat it. I'm so sorry." Everyone stares at me. "I have serious stomach trouble, you know, and the vermicelli noodles soak up so much oil when you fry them! You do fry them before you add them to the pilaf?" Nods from the women. "I'm sure it's delicious, but I can't digest the oil."

Missak is silent for a few seconds. Then he bursts out, "But Hannah, I wonder if *toasting* the noodles in the oven would work out better for you? It would be worth a try, don't you think? No frying, no oil, no indigestion. Right?"

We all laughed and nodded in agreement, and I tucked away the added thought that toasted noodles would also stay crisp if you wanted to store them. But I didn't realize, sitting at that dinner table, what a monumental change in my life would follow from the seed of that conversation.

It began later that night at Jack's house. I've retired early but I can't get to sleep. Something is boiling up inside my brain. It's like a hot spring bubbling closer and closer to the surface. At eleven PM I jump out of bed, run into the living room, and spout it out.

"Jack, Lorraine! I'm going to start a business! I'm going to put my pilaf on the market! My own pilaf mix!"

Jack laughs. "Sure, Mom. You'll be famous. For tonight, though, better get some sleep."

Laurie sees something in my eyes. She gets up and hugs me.

"I think you'll do it, Mom. I believe you'll really do it!"

When I get back to Worcester, George too seems skeptical. Maybe it takes a woman to see within a person, to know when someone has crossed an invisible line and there's no turning back. Maybe it's just that George has a new worry of his own.

"You know what I found out while you were gone?" He sits me down at the lunch counter. "In the second phase of this reconstruction of the Square, they're going to re-route Lincoln Street. And do you know what that means? We'll wind up on a dead-end street!"

I cover his hands. "Don't worry, George. Plenty of people will still find their way to our store. We'll manage, I promise."

Then, when I've made him smile at this reversal of our usual attitudes, I look him in the eye. "But from now on," I say, "it's your lunchroom exclusively."

"And what will you be doing?"

"I'll be upstairs figuring out how you package a pilaf mix."

"Figuring?"

"And cooking, George. Pilaf after pilaf after pilaf. 'Til

we get it exactly right, Carol and I."

The plan works pretty well. George goes wild in the lunchroom in his own creative way. And I send down my experimental mixes anytime he asks. Somebody has to test the mix!

Upstairs, Carol and I try every variation we can invent. How much garlic? Which spices do we accent? Is it too salty? Too bland? What about meat stock? Is there a suitable powdered bouillon available? Several. Which brand? Will we ever get the mix the same way twice?

I even slip upstairs with a couple of competitors' rice mixtures under my arm. Let's check out what we'll have to conquer in the marketplace.

We have a sampling session one morning.

"Nothing to worry about, as far as I can tell," I decide, spoon in hand. "What do you think, Carol?"

"They can't compare, Mom."

"But will mine sell?"

"All you have to do is get yours on the shelves, Mom!"

We did a little dance around the kitchen and returned to the problem at hand, which was, again, the vermicelli noodles.

The vermicelli toasted well in the oven and stayed crisp, as we had hoped, indefinitely. But it was a slow, awkward method, and we missed the flavor of the oil. I found the answer when I went to our beautiful Armenian Church of Our Savior one cold winter evening. An unexpected solution. After the service I dutifully sample the copious offerings of Armenian foods on the buffet table. Familiar. Delicious!

But wait a minute! One of the pilafs is different. What is it? The rice is the same. Ah, it's the noodles. Not vermicelli. Brown and crisp, with a hint of oil. A nut-like taste. What is it?

"It's called *orzo*," the woman tells me, when I track her down in the kitchen.

And it works! We find we can quick-fry the orzo, a wheat pasta shaped like small ovals, on top of the stove. The oil coats it but doesn't sink in! And it stays crisp. How long? Days. Weeks. It's still crisp on the shelf, and nutty delicious. Amen to that problem!

Between experiments my unpredictable body asserted its own priorities and slowed us down, but finally the time came for full commitment. Washington's Birthday, 1962. I take down a pot of pilaf made from our purest, most perfect mix, and serve it at George's lunch counter.

One of our bar stool customers is a regular, a patent lawyer named Norman Blodgett. I watch him as he eats.

"What do you think?" I demand. "Can I market this successfully? It's made from my own package mix."

He nods slowly, then gives me the thumbs up sign.

"Yes," he says. Then louder, "You can do it, Hannah!"

Then, while I'm still concentrating on his face, he grins, "Not only can you sell it, but just think, Hannah, if you sell just one box of pilaf mix to every family in the United States, you may change the palates of an entire country!"

Applause up and down the counter. I marched upstairs with new fire in my eyes.

It took us nine months from that day to launch our company, NEAR EAST FOOD PRODUCTS. What a gestation period that was! What an education I squeezed out for myself! How I haunted the library! How I begged, cajoled, and demanded information from a hundred sources. But energy now soared through my body, and at night my brain gnawed endlessly at the day's problems.

Some of the answers only complicated our efforts. For instance, we discovered that there is no such thing as a patent on a food product. Anyone can imitate or copy you at will. Well, no time to worry about that now. Then there were the many questions about shelf life of the ingredients. Later we found a lab in Boston which officially tested each item, but first I spent many days talking by phone with Food and Drug staff people in Washington, D.C., and with other agencies to which they referred me, across the country. I'll never forget how helpful and encouraging they all were to this fifty-two-year-old newcomer. Especially helpful was a man in California who always seemed to come up with answers. Putting it all together, I learned about legalities, sources of supply, performance testing, and suitability of the various ingredients which we wanted to use.

Then there arose the challenge of finding local wholesalers, or buying from wholesalers at a distance, because a fledgling company needs to cut corners. That meant avoiding buying in small quantities, whether it was the foil bags we first used, glue, spices, bulghur, or rice.

The kitchen of our apartment becomes our laboratory. The pace quickens. Carol and I, and Cohar, who now commutes from Connecticut to help us, work single-mindedly. How strong should our foil bags be? One pouch or two for each mix? How do we word the recipe? Is it simple, foolproof? What could go wrong with our dehydration techniques? How can we measure exactly? Endless questions, endless ferreting out of answers.

I remember so well the day we set up our first crude production line. Sitting on the floor in the living room is a little boy busily opening foil bags and passing them on to his mother and father, next in line at the various tables which are staggered through to the kitchen. The little boy is Marc, the son of our nephew Marcel and his wife Lee. Also at attention on the line are two wonderful neighbors, Peg Lee and Lil Kasper, and finally our own family.

Hannah Kalajian (seated, center) and family, Christmas,
1945. Clockwise from left: son Jack, daughter Cohar,
husband George, and daughter Carol.

The Near
East logo
and
boxes.

The bags march raggedly onward. Ingredients are carefully measured, knifed off clean from cup or spoon, and dropped in. At the end of the line, the warm glue is spread, and the sealed bags line up like soldiers, in a succession of trays which were designed to hold flats of spring planting. We joke, laugh, and drink coffee during five-minute breaks and rub sore muscles and tired feet at the end of the day. I suppose all entrepreneurs who start on a shoestring remember fondly the early days and the crew that worked together then.

One last problem. Boxes. We are lucky. We find a Worcester firm, the Mead Box Company, which designs the perfect box for us. In the beginning we were motivated mostly by price concerns, but it worked so well that we've never changed the design. It's a two-color package. Dark brown lettering on a white background. A logo, top center, which spells NEAR EAST in exotically curved letters which hint of camels and desert sands. A sheaf of golden wheat winds up along the left-hand side. We bought it for its low cost, but we've kept it ever since because it stands out beautifully on the shelves, striking in its simplicity. The sheaf of wheat has never left the box. It merely changed colors as our products proliferated.

But I'm getting ahead of myself. Before we dropped the first bag of mix into a box, I decided, impulsively, to test our virgin product in the real marketplace. My target: Boston.

14
Marketing

IT is late fall, 1963. Our fledgling product faces a chilly christening. George and I are driving to Boston. He's at the wheel and I'm beside him, gearing myself up like a soldier facing his first battle. The back seat holds my armor: two plastic gardening trays packed with foil bags (one tray full of wheat pilaf mix, the other rice) and beside the trays an electric saucepan and an apron.

I have wangled an appointment, at noon, with John Mugar, president of the Star Market chain founded by his cousin, Stephen P. Mugar. There are forty Star Markets in New England, but Boston is the keystone.

At 11:50 AM I clatter into John Mugar's office, ready to establish a beachhead.

"Well, yes, there's a kitchen, of sorts, right in there, Mrs. Kalajian. Take it over if you want," says Mugar, a bit bewildered. He waves an arm toward an adjoining room.

I hustle in, find an electrical outlet, and twenty minutes later Mugar is standing in the doorway, breathing in the aromatic steam and looking hungry. Minutes later he's grinning over a plate of Near East Wheat Pilaf.

"It's wonderful! Delicious, Hannah—may I call you Hannah?"

I nod, speechless, because I'm taking a deep, deep breath.

"You have some more with you, don't you? Two kinds, the Wheat and Rice? Leave them all with me and I'll get them right on the shelves!"

We have a foothold! I float down the stairs and into the car. During the following weeks and months the Star Market in Boston gobbles up load after load of Near East mixes, and we quickly acquire "facings" for our new boxes in all thirty-nine other Star Markets. After all, if Boston likes it, it must be good!

That first winter both my daughters worked heroically at marketing. Cohar spent day after day spinning her wheels through the slush and ice of countless New England towns. It's wonderful how doors open once you have "references": "Yes, we're doing very well in the Star Markets, you know . . ." After she hit them with that opener, she'd get an okay to set up a demonstration. You know how it goes: the card table, the rows of little paper cups, people clustering around the tantalizing aroma. M-m-m, what is this? It's different . . . but good, very good. Their enthusiasm always energizes Cohar magically, no matter how tired she is.

Our first trickle of success grows to a stream. They *like* us. First National accepts us, Iandoli's, the A & P, New England Grocers, Stop and Shop, Purity Supreme. Something wonderful is happening.

Meantime, back in our bedroom office, Carol is quietly and persistently widening our markets in her own way. She has acquired a list of every cooking editor of every U.S. newspaper big enough to have a cooking editor. Day after day she sends out letters to them, accompanied by several sample boxes. On another front she tackles every major distributor of food products, again through the mails: "We believe you will have the same success with our products that our New England grocers are enjoying. Please accept this sample case for trial distribution . . ." She has no idea whether this low-budget advertising will succeed in time to keep us out of the red, but she never stops, never loses patience.

By mid-February we are doing enough business to make the decision to incorporate. George has lost his initial cynicism and enters in the heady spirit of success. NEAR EAST Food Products, Inc. I'm beginning to feel overwhelmed, but I'm too busy to worry about it. A family corporation!

We have six women helping us now, along with the family. The bedroom stores hundred of cases. Our rag-tag production line advances like an irrepressible lava flow, taking over the dining room, then the living room. The initial output of twenty-five cases a day increases to fifty, a hundred, a hundred and fifty. Two hundred!

"Are you ready to give up the grocery side of the store for a production center?" I challenge George one morning. "We're bursting out of the house!"

Startled, he sees that I'm serious. He shrugs his shoulders, grins, and dances me around the luncheonette.

"I give up! I yield to the inevitable! But promise me you'll provide my side with a constant supply of pilaf, because I'm introducing a new item to my customers. A *pilaf sub*!"

A new sign appears across the front of our store. Using the NEAR EAST logo from our box, it announces that "George's" is the "Home of the Original Near East Rice Pilaf." We all stand out there and admire it. A proud team. Yet I know that it may be several years before profits exceed expenditures. Increased demand means more employees, more space, more equipment, and improved controls. That's the way it is for infant companies. My friendly business advisors have warned me of this, especially our good neighbor, the Morgan Construction Company, and the Worcester Chamber of Commerce.

By summer, Cohar, who has moved to Worcester with her family, has formally joined the corporation. She and I combine forces to invade the New York market. We manage to get one corner of a booth at the week-long Food Fair at the Coliseum. Bravely, we set up our table and plug in the saucepans. Miraculous! Every surge of bodies pushing out of the elevators brings a line of "samplers" who have followed their own noses to our bubbling pots, like children following the Pied Piper.

We march on, conquering Gimbel's, then the prestigious Gristede's. S. S. Pierce asks us for a demonstration. Every favorable response gives us new ammunition. We encounter little trouble getting a booth at the annual Macy's Food Fair. There our surest weapon, the aroma of steaming pilaf, lures customers from every corner of the store.

Immediate rewards fed back to us from our stints at Macy's and the Coliseum Food Fair. Food editors who roam these fairs carried the lingering taste of our samples back to their desks and began to highlight the mixes in their columns.

Intoxicating stuff. We feel like stage performers. Packing the car and hitting the highway starts the energy build-up. It peaks through the demonstration and yields to fatigue only late at night when we stretch out in a strange hotel room, shedding our shoes, munching on deli sandwiches, aching for sleep, but still chattering compulsively about the day's small triumphs.

No sales or promotional successes can compare, however, to one special joy: the fan letters that began to trickle in. Letters are hands reaching out to you, voices speaking directly to you, strangers touching your inner self. I've kept them all, and even now I sort through them sometimes, savoring the original joy and pride each time.

"I tasted your pilaf mix when I was visiting my son in New Hampshire during the summer. It was just so delicious! But I've looked for it down here in South Carolina and none of our markets carry it. Do you suppose you'll spread to our area soon?"

"I usually don't write to food companies, but I must tell you that your mix went over so big with our family! And believe me I've got five fussy eaters . . ."

"I was a die-hard when it came to instant mixes, but you've converted me. It doesn't taste like a mix at all . . ."

"Mrs. Kalajian, I'm glad your name is right on the box. I feel as if I know you . . ."

And one from Australia! ". . . and I don't suppose we'll ever get your product over here on the other side of the world, but if you ever do sell here, I'll be an enthusiastic promoter!"

The lady from Australia had tried our rice pilaf when she visited California. We had our food friend and first client, John Mugar, to thank for our early outlet in the western United States, because he recommended the NEAR EAST Food Products to the Jewel Tea chain, which stretched from California eastward to Chicago and New York.

I wasn't the only one getting letters. Carol also began to reap the rewards of her prodigious outpouring of mail to food editors. Small paragraphs, even entire articles, praised the quality and ease of our two mixes. Some sent copies of the write-ups, which Carol promptly copied in turn and enclosed in her letters to distributors.

Events tumbled over themselves. Sometime in the late

sixties, Jack came back to Massachusetts with his family. He stands in the doorway and runs his eyes over our hands-on production line. My own eyes feast on him. Jackie. My son. Welcome home.

"Nice sign, out front." He tosses his head back a bit. "How's it going, girls? Pretty frantic pace here, eh? Each box custom packed? Classy-y-y!"

"Don't tease, Jack," I say. "We could use a little engineering help. Your sister Cohar has set up a system of rollers, over here, see, to carry the pouches along as they're filled, but it's true we do a lot of hand work."

"I was just kidding, Mom," he laughs. "And I'll be glad to help if I can." He throws his arm around me. "But I do have a full-time engineering job in Waltham."

"You could figure out a way to close the flaps on these boxes automatically, maybe?" Cohar interrupts from the far end of the line.

In the next few weeks Jack answers that challenge ingeniously, with the aid of two old sewing machine motors and several mechanical arms. It looks like an Andy Warhol exhibit, but it works. The box slides across, the arms swing—zap, zip—and all four flaps slide together in perfect alignment. Cheers!

In a few months Jack is sold on the company and decides to stay on. He is sprouting new ideas, envisioning other products, wider markets, and before too long, bigger space. It's almost ten years since I handed a sample dish of wheat pilaf to John Mugar in Boston. I feel the speed of this ride we're on, and leisure hours on Thompson Pond become more precious, as the grandchildren swell to number—what is it now?—six, with another coming soon.

1971. Jack has a proposition.

"Mom, how about sitting back and enjoying life as the owner and chief consultant of this company? Let us run it for you. You deserve it. What do you say?

"And you will still be in demand as the expert tester of new products," he adds, flashing his persuasive grin.

I agree, without any real reservations. George needs me; his health is precarious now. And it will be wonderful to watch my grandchildren growing up.

Even so, on the day that Jack takes over as president, with Cohar becoming vice-president and Carol the treasurer, I sit for a while in the car, my eyes fixed on the block letters of our company sign below the familiar "George's Market." Events are moving so quickly that I need time to let my emotions catch up to reality.

If I had any worries about time on my hands at home, however, they disappear instantly. The company keeps me very busy intensively testing new products. Jack loves to make deadlines: Mom, I need a feasibility answer on Lentil Pilaf Mix (or the new Spanish Rice, or bouillon) by next week, how about it? Out would come the rows of pots, the succession of taste tests, almost like 1962, a lifetime ago.

At the same time I discover an additional outlet for my restless energy, one which enriches my life for years. I study the art of painting and find that making a picture come to life on canvas satisfies my soul in a new and beautiful way. So retirement is never complete. Meanwhile, the company forges ahead.

*

*   *

By the start of 1972 the inevitable happens. The corporation is outgrowing the store. A dozen employees put up about three hundred cases a day in cramped quarters, and business has long since turned the profit corner, grossing several hundred thousands of dollars a year.

Bigger space is an easy problem. The company's new

Store front, George's Spa, first home of Near East Pilaf
Mix, 1963. Work crew outside, with Hannah at far left.

Inside, the first assembly line. Left to right, Claudia
Markarian, Elizabeth Chakarian, Ely Bardo, and Hannah.

Hannah Kalajian at the new quarters, 1974.
(Photo: Worcester Telegram)

home is a huge warehouse at 95 Prescott Street, only a half mile from "George's." I come in on the first few days to help the team scrub, scrape, and soak off the oily residue of previous tenants. This process I'm accustomed to, but the empty space is awesome.

"It'll take a lot of production to fill this place," I muse out loud, leaning on a long-handled mop. I'd be happier back in the womb, at the market.

"Where do you want these sacks of rice, Jack?" yells Carol from the outside platform where a huge trailor-truck disgorges supplies.

Cohar walks over to me with a wide smile. "Don't worry, Mom, we'll do it here, like we did it back there, only bigger and better."

Frenzied activity follows. Jack hustles to choose, adapt, or design automatic machines. Soon the new machinery is humming away, its arms dropping measured ingredients into pouches, its metal plates compressing glued surfaces, its belts and pulleys whisking pouches along to meet boxes, its chutes loading boxes neatly into cases.

Production doubles without adding new employees. Business publications are taking note of us. Profiles of our evolution appear in local and state papers. Competitors feel us out on selling the corporation. Very complimentary, but no thanks!

Carol, our goodwill ambassador, now married, is having children of her own, but she sticks by the corporation. Everyone helps take care of the grandchildren in their special area at the back of the shop.

Food fairs still take us women out on the road during this period. I love these trips. I love sharing the comradeship with my daughters. And we keep adding new clients: Bond Foods, Buy-Rite, restaurant chains.

The office mail still brings the personal letters I love. A

special one arrives in '74 after a local article about NEAR EAST. It gives me great pleasure:

> Dear Hannah,
>
> That was an excellent biography of you in yesterday's *Telegram* [the *Worcester Sunday Telegram*]. Your courage and your spirit were very evident ... and I am glad that all has turned out so successfully, and that your children are running the business you founded. With best wishes, I remain
>
> Sincerely,
>
> Bill Sawyer
> (William H. Sawyer)
> [President of Sawyer Lumber Co.]

The year 1978 brought us a personal loss which shattered us all. On the first day of spring, as the golden forsythia heralded new life everywhere in New England, George died.

Carol and I are visiting in California when he goes. We have moved George, temporarily, into a nursing home until I return. Cohar sits with him almost every night. On Friday evening he seems restless.

"When will Mommy be back?" he asks, with an almost child-like intensity which pulls his head up from the pillow.

"Don't worry, Daddy, she's flying back Sunday." Cohar reaches for the hands gripping the white bedspread.

"No, no! That's too late. Too late."

George's premonition proves true. During the night his exhausted heart stops beating. The little boy who survived the wild dogs of the sheik's compound has finally surrendered his spirit.

As soon as I see the family standing solemnly in line at the airport to greet me, I know what has happened.

Later, standing beside his casket, I look at the thin face against the satin lining and remember when we were young together. Sleep, my dearest. You fought well. Now rest.

These first dozen or so years of NEAR EAST's growth into healthy adolescence remain the zenith of my dreams. I have felt like an adventurer on a raft, riding the Colorado, swept by currents, knocking against rocks, plunging through white water, tense and alive, focused on the next bend in the river, and committed to whatever lay ahead.

15
Near East Comes of Age

TIME begins to slow down for me after 1972, while the company gathers ever more speed in its headlong development. Several years later, when I finally decide to sell the business to the children, it's with the conviction that my dream has come of age, and now it should belong to the second generation.

The rest of the story is theirs, and it is a miracle tale in itself.

*

*   *

1975: NEAR EAST Food Products, Inc., builds a 9,000-square-foot building in Jytek Park in Leominster. The 9,000 square feet grow soon to 14,000. New markets open up, many of them restaurant chains: Magic Pan, Marriott, Red Lobster, Steak and Ale, Legal Seafoods, and others. The armed forces quietly contract for our products. Employees and staff swell to seventy-two.

*

*   *

1984: NEAR EAST moves to a 46,000-square-foot area off Route 117 in Leominster. Our new facility offers the luxuries of an indoor racquetball court, exercise rooms, and saunas. The products number fifteen now, including Wheat, Rice, and Lentil pilafs, Spanish Rice, Tabouleh, Couscous, Sesame Tahini, Falafel, and others. The distinctive white box with its color-coded spray of wheat has not changed, but the advertising is expensive and slick, appearing routinely in national magazines and television. Markets spread to Canada, Australia, and Europe. At the Los Angeles Olympics the athletes enjoy Near East's Couscous as well as its Wheat Pilaf.

*

*   *

1986: My baby has grown strong and prosperous, beyond anything I ever dreamed. Now a multi-million-dollar business, it has attracted many would-be buyers. One of them makes a bid which writes a final chapter, not for NEAR EAST Foods, but for our family corporation. On December 30th, 1986, NEAR EAST acquires a new owner: the H. J. Heinz Company. Jack will stay during the transition period, so that the products will maintain the same high quality as before.

I look back with humility and wonder that a thirteen-year-old immigrant girl could grow up to affect the eating habits of her entire adopted country and that a Wednesday night luncheonette special could become the embodiment of the American dream.

Epilogue

"WELL, that's the story. You've heard it all."
The last interview is over. All the milestones of my life lie captured on the half-dozen tapes my friend carries home with her.

I sit, folded into the green armchair, watching the October light slant lower against the windows. Around me the ghosts of the past still hover. I'm reluctant to let them go.

"You see? It all turned out okay!"

I laugh. Here I am talking out loud to a roomful of ghosts. It did turn out well, though. My life was such a crazy obstacle course, but just when I was ready to settle for a no-win finish, out cropped that stubborn drive again and I found myself giving birth to an infant business. I mothered it through childhood. Then, when I put the business in the hands of my children, it was like sending a teenager off to college. You want him to be independent, but you still live his problems and share his triumphs.

My brainchild's success has dazzled me at times. I remember going to the elegant receptions our company would give to announce a new product, or a new location. I'd try to sit in a quiet corner or against the wall, overwhelmed by the magnitude of it. Was it real? Did I start all this? Would it suddenly disappear like the light on a movie screen when the last credits roll by? I'd watch my children and grandchildren move about the reception area with the grace and assurance that comes with economic security. A tremendous satisfaction.

Now I sit here wondering how my children feel as they face the future. Will they still be "teammates" without the corporation to hold them together? Do they miss the early days, at the lake? Do they miss George, as I do? Do they still hear his stories and his laughter, in the night silences? Do they harbor any hurts, unarticulated, from the childhood years?

I want to tell them something: nothing matters, not yesterday's struggles nor today's good fortune; nothing matters except the will to keep going. You are all members of one of the most persistent, proud races on earth. We don't accept endings, only new beginnings. When I was fifty years old, I was a broken woman. At fifty-two I started a whole new life. Whatever new beginnings lie ahead for you, my children, go to meet them joyously and unafraid.